WITHDRAWN
FROM THE COLLECTION OF
SACRAMENTO PUBLIC LIBRARY

"revolutionary" – **Mookc**

"One of the first great comics…up there with *Watchmen, V for Vendetta, Dark Knight*…The things that we talk about when we talk about comics, Halo Jones should have been one of them." – **Neil Gaiman**

"Alan Moore's greatest comic book creation … a superb character study, an especially important book for teenage girls to read. In a world of increasing insecurity, not only politically but personally (body image, place in society, material wealth, sense of self), Halo Jones offers a critique of, and a refuge from, the absurdities of an uncertain world."
– Tribe

"Halo Jones was my first love. Or maybe my first role model. The girl that got out." – **Lauren Beukes**

"the story of an ordinary woman, not a superhero or special snowflake, but a woman who made her own story … a character that represented the everywoman … *The Ballad of Halo Jones* broke the mould … remarkably timeless" – **The Independent**

"groundbreaking feminist heroine … one of the comic industry's strongest role models" – **The Guardian**

"exponentially cooler than knock-offs like *Tank Girl*, mostly because she remains a fed-up real person amid the wild space opera of her universe" – **Empire**

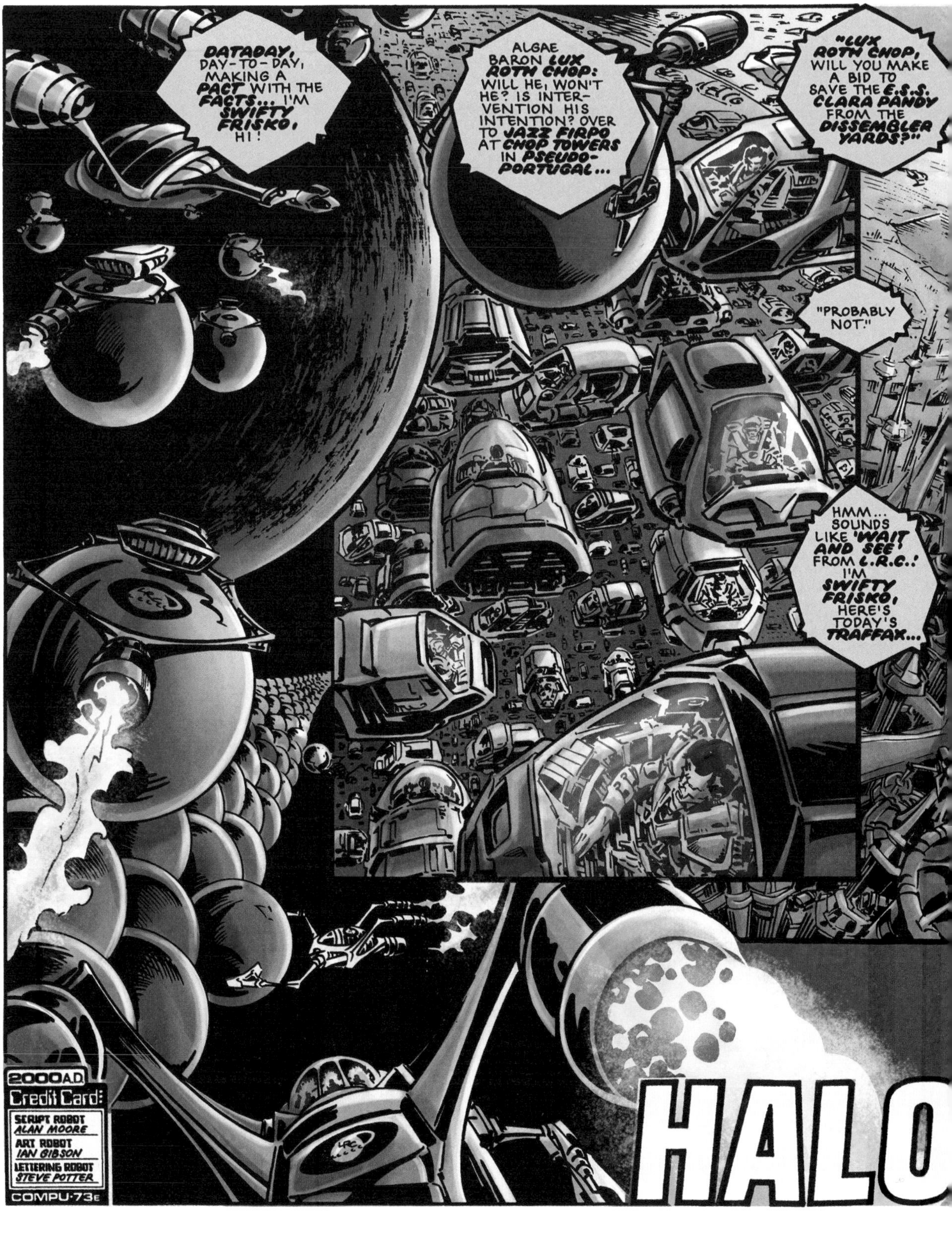
DATADAY, DAY-TO-DAY, MAKING A PACT WITH THE FACTS... I'M SWIFTY FRISKO, HI!
ALGAE BARON LUX ROTH CHOP: WILL HE, WON'T HE? IS INTERVENTION HIS INTENTION? OVER TO JAZZ FIRPO AT CHOP TOWERS IN PSEUDO-PORTUGAL...
"LUX ROTH CHOP, WILL YOU MAKE A BID TO SAVE THE E.S.S. CLARA PANDY FROM THE DISSEMBLER YARDS?"
"PROBABLY NOT."
HMM... SOUNDS LIKE 'WAIT AND SEE' FROM L.R.C.! I'M SWIFTY FRISKO, HERE'S TODAY'S TRAFFAX...
2000 A.D.
Credit Card:
SCRIPT ROBOT ALAN MOORE
ART ROBOT IAN GIBSON
LETTERING ROBOT STEVE POTTER
COMPU-73E
HALO

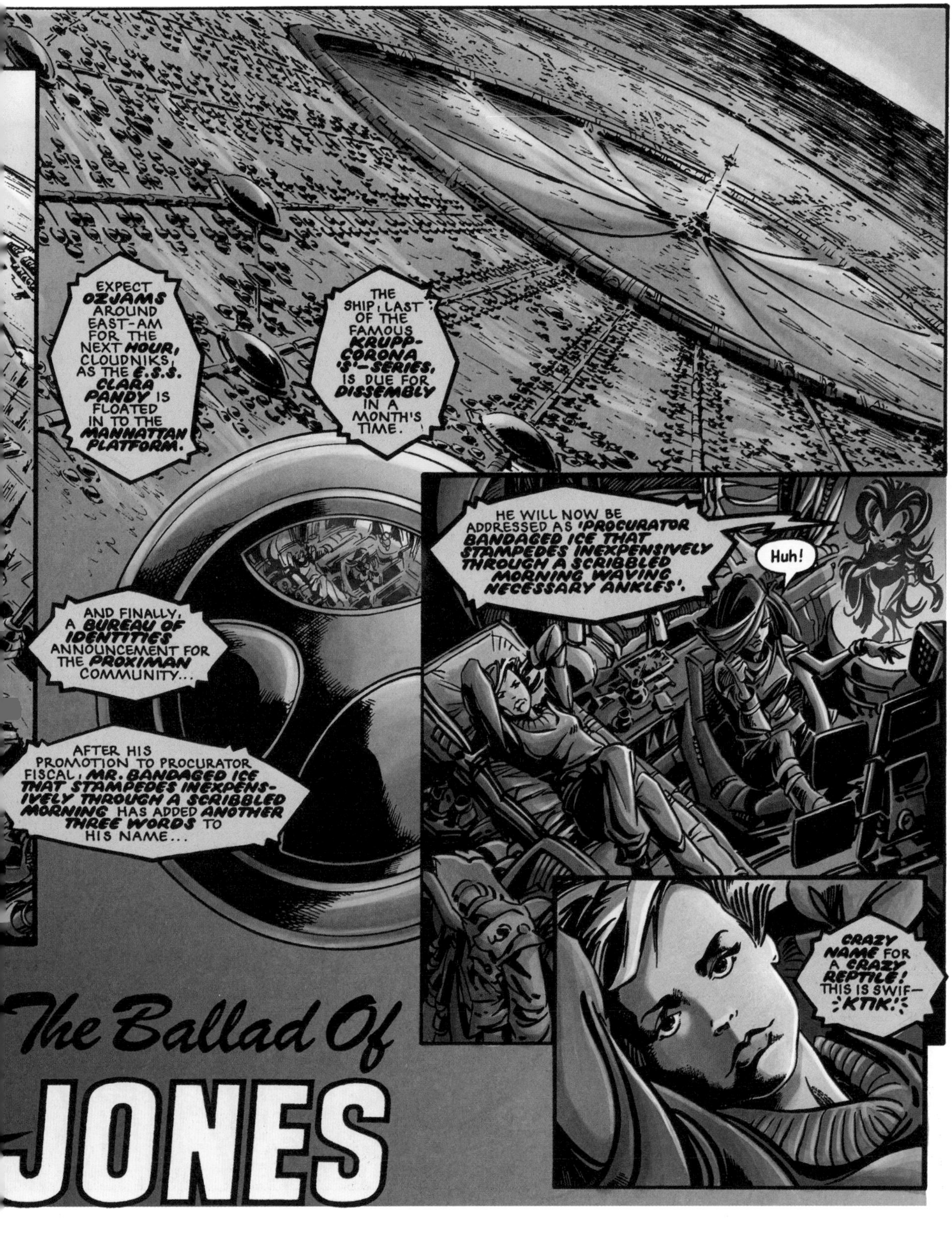
EXPECT OZJAMS AROUND EAST-AM FOR THE NEXT HOUR, CLOUDNIKS, AS THE E.S.S. CLARA PANDY IS FLOATED IN TO THE MANNATTAN PLATFORM.
THE SHIP, LAST OF THE FAMOUS KRUPP-CORONA 'S'-SERIES, IS DUE FOR DISSEMBLY IN A MONTH'S TIME.
AND FINALLY, A BUREAU OF IDENTITIES ANNOUNCEMENT FOR THE PROXIMAN COMMUNITY...
AFTER HIS PROMOTION TO PROCURATOR FISCAL, MR. BANDAGED ICE THAT STAMPEDES INEXPENS-IVELY THROUGH A SCRIBBLED MORNING HAS ADDED ANOTHER THREE WORDS TO HIS NAME...
HE WILL NOW BE ADDRESSED AS 'PROCURATOR BANDAGED ICE THAT STAMPEDES INEXPENSIVELY THROUGH A SCRIBBLED MORNING WAVING NECESSARY ANKLES'.
Huh!
CRAZY NAME FOR A CRAZY REPTILE! THIS IS SWIF-
KTIK!
The Ballad Of
JONES

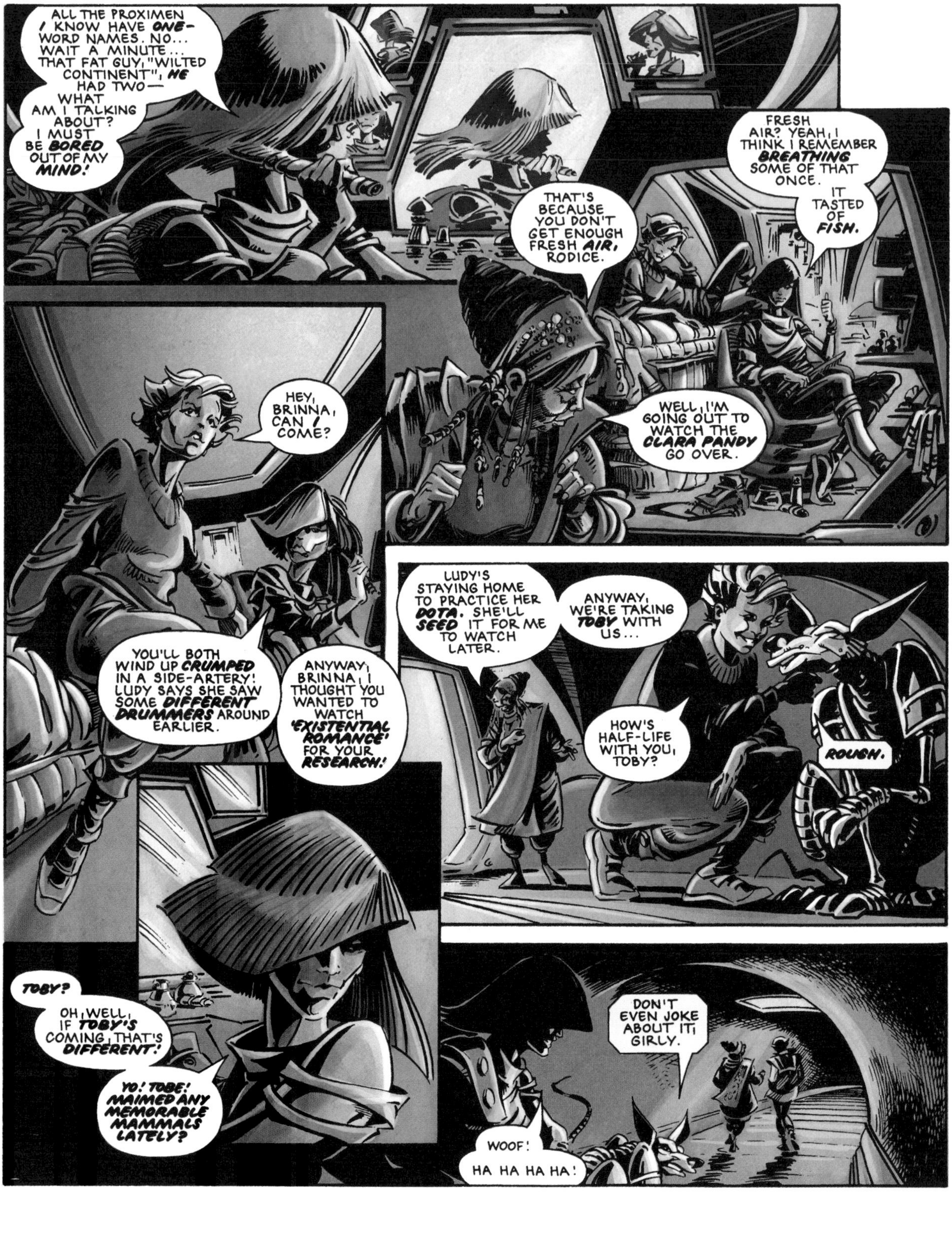
ALL THE PROXIMEN I KNOW HAVE ONE-WORD NAMES. NO... WAIT A MINUTE... THAT FAT GUY, "WILTED CONTINENT", HE HAD TWO— WHAT AM I TALKING ABOUT? I MUST BE BORED OUT OF MY MIND!
FRESH AIR? YEAH, I THINK I REMEMBER BREATHING SOME OF THAT ONCE.
IT TASTED OF FISH.
THAT'S BECAUSE YOU DON'T GET ENOUGH FRESH AIR, RODICE.
WELL, I'M GOING OUT TO WATCH THE CLARA PANDY GO OVER.
HEY, BRINNA, CAN I COME?
YOU'LL BOTH WIND UP CRUMPED IN A SIDE-ARTERY! LUDY SAYS SHE SAW SOME DIFFERENT DRUMMERS AROUND EARLIER.
ANYWAY, BRINNA, I THOUGHT YOU WANTED TO WATCH 'EXISTENTIAL ROMANCE' FOR YOUR RESEARCH!
LUDY'S STAYING HOME TO PRACTICE HER DOTA. SHE'LL SEED IT FOR ME TO WATCH LATER.
ANYWAY, WE'RE TAKING TOBY WITH US...
HOW'S HALF-LIFE WITH YOU, TOBY?
ROUGH.
TOBY?
OH, WELL, IF TOBY'S COMING, THAT'S DIFFERENT!
YO! TOBE! MAIMED ANY MEMORABLE MAMMALS LATELY?
DON'T EVEN JOKE ABOUT IT, GIRLY.
WOOF!
HA HA HA HA!

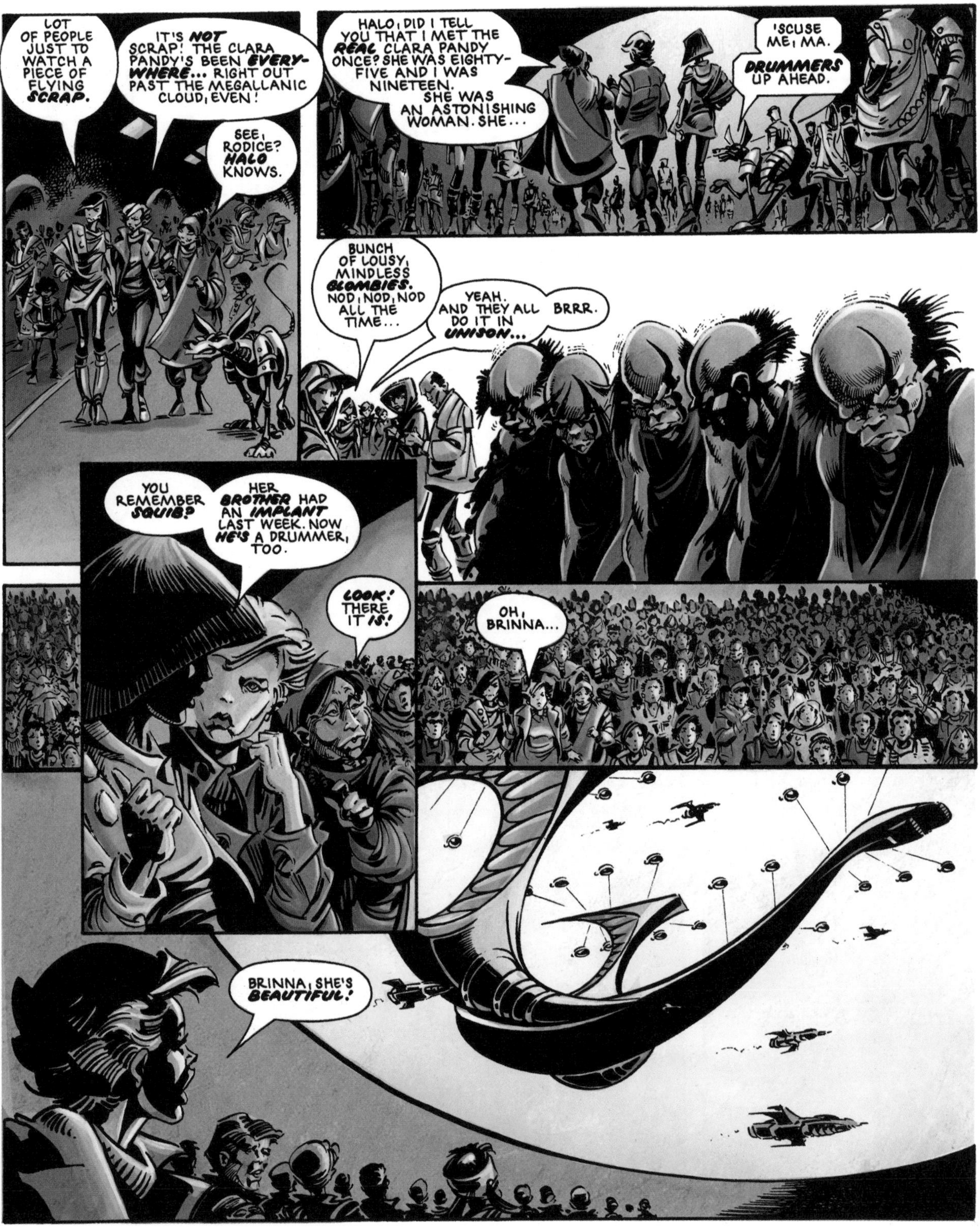

LOT OF PEOPLE JUST TO WATCH A PIECE OF FLYING SCRAP.
IT'S NOT SCRAP! THE CLARA PANDY'S BEEN EVERY-WHERE... RIGHT OUT PAST THE MEGALLANIC CLOUD, EVEN!
SEE, RODICE? HALO KNOWS.
HALO, DID I TELL YOU THAT I MET THE REAL CLARA PANDY ONCE? SHE WAS EIGHTY-FIVE AND I WAS NINETEEN. SHE WAS AN ASTONISHING WOMAN. SHE...
'SCUSE ME, MA. DRUMMERS UP AHEAD.
BUNCH OF LOUSY, MINDLESS GLOMBIES. NOD, NOD, NOD ALL THE TIME...
YEAH. AND THEY ALL DO IT IN UNISON...
BRRR.
YOU REMEMBER SQUIB?
HER BROTHER HAD AN IMPLANT LAST WEEK. NOW HE'S A DRUMMER, TOO.
LOOK! THERE IT IS!
OH, BRINNA...
BRINNA, SHE'S BEAUTIFUL!

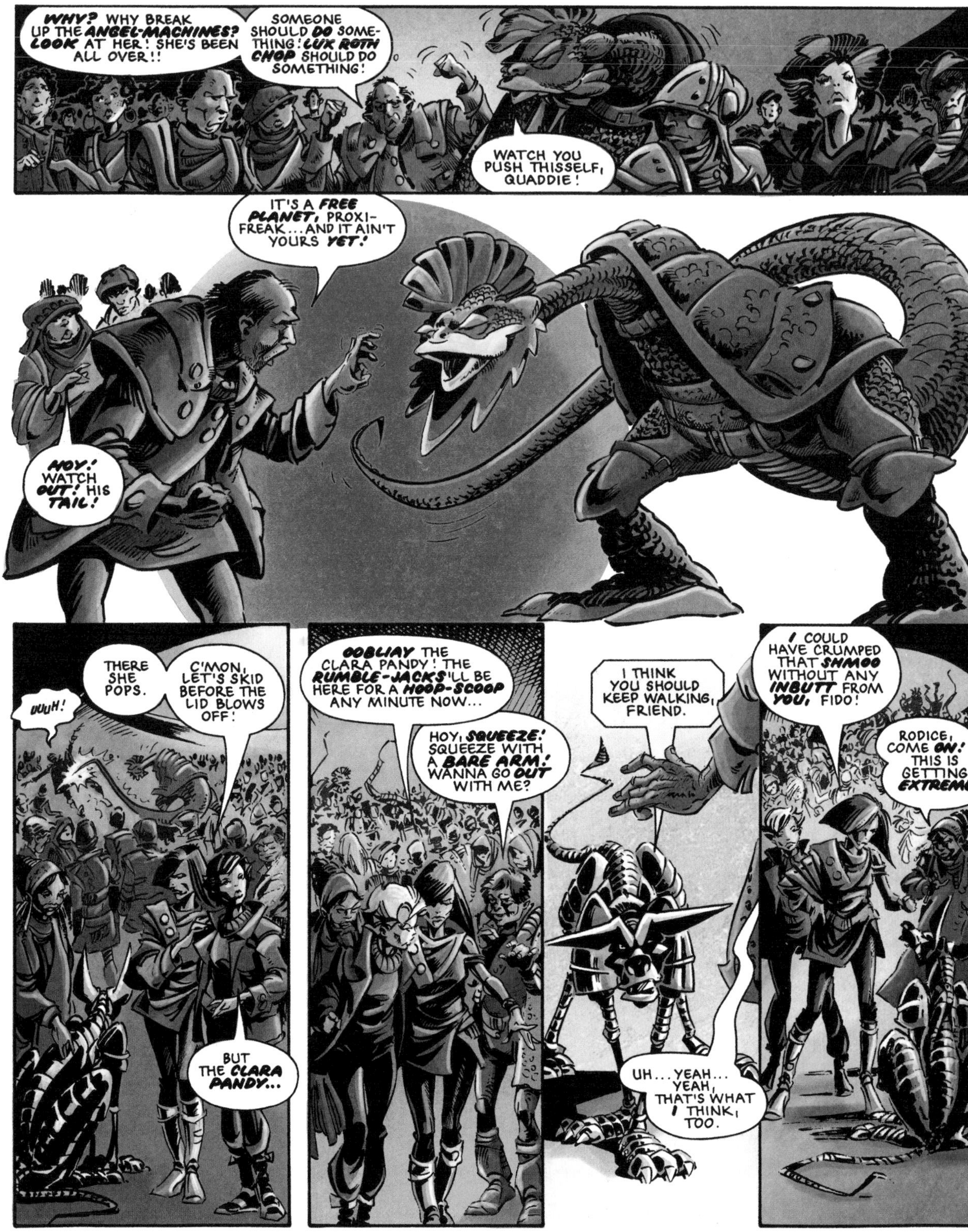
WHY? WHY BREAK UP THE ANGEL-MACHINES? LOOK AT HER! SHE'S BEEN ALL OVER!!
SOMEONE SHOULD DO SOMETHING! LUX ROTH CHOP SHOULD DO SOMETHING!
WATCH YOU PUSH THISSELF, QUADDIE!
IT'S A FREE PLANET, PROXI-FREAK... AND IT AIN'T YOURS YET!
HOY! WATCH OUT! HIS TAIL!
UUUH!
THERE SHE POPS.
C'MON, LET'S SKID BEFORE THE LID BLOWS OFF!
BUT THE CLARA PANDY...
OOBLIAY THE CLARA PANDY! THE RUMBLE-JACKS'LL BE HERE FOR A HOOP-SCOOP ANY MINUTE NOW...
HOY, SQUEEZE! SQUEEZE WITH A BARE ARM! WANNA GO OUT WITH ME?
I THINK YOU SHOULD KEEP WALKING, FRIEND.
UH... YEAH... YEAH, THAT'S WHAT I THINK, TOO.
I COULD HAVE CRUMPED THAT SHMOO WITHOUT ANY INBUTT FROM YOU, FIDO!
RODICE, COME ON! THIS IS GETTING EXTREME!

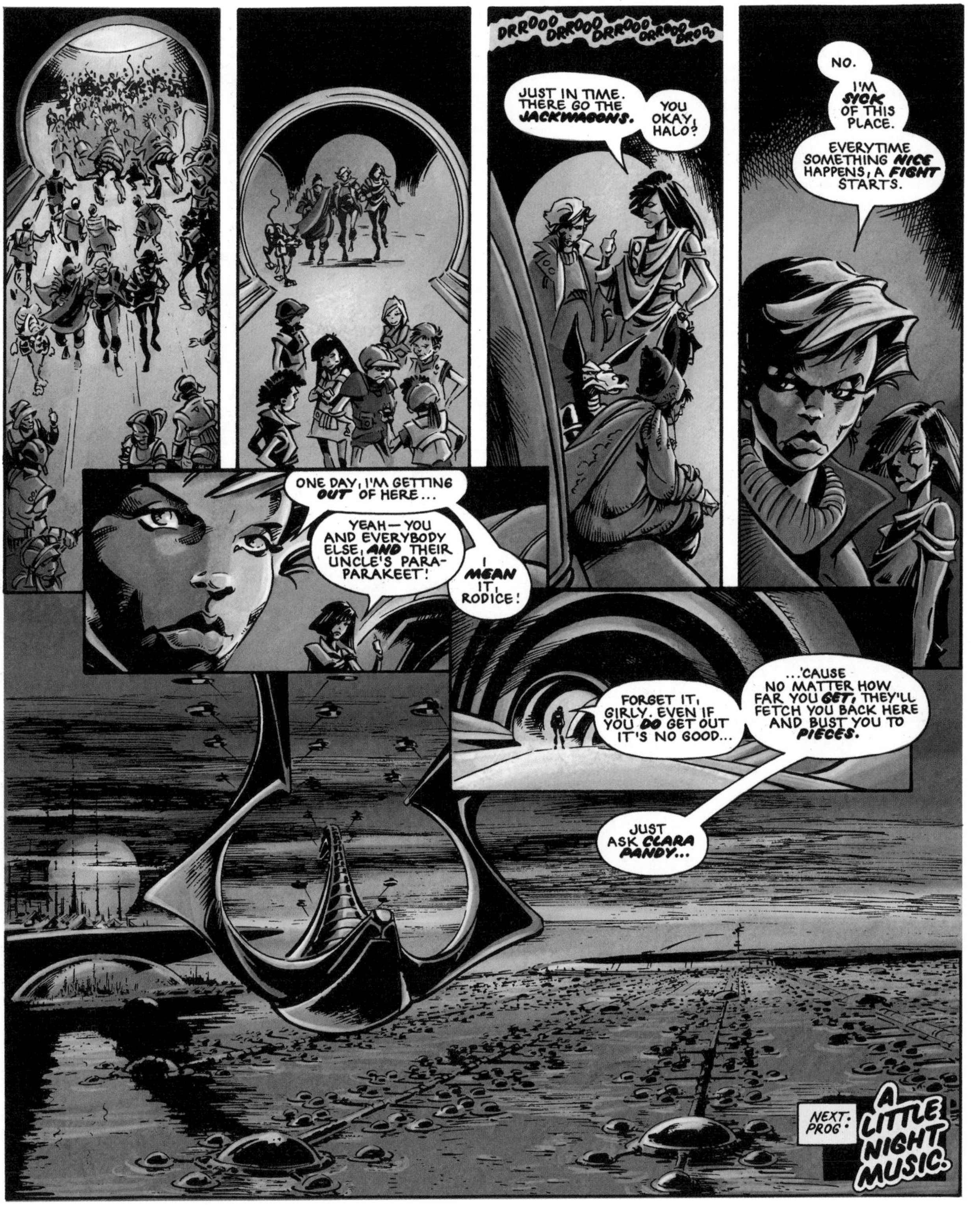

DRROOO DRROOO DRROOO DRROOO DROOO
JUST IN TIME. THERE GO THE JACKWAGONS.
YOU OKAY, HALO?
NO.
I'M SICK OF THIS PLACE.
EVERYTIME SOMETHING NICE HAPPENS, A FIGHT STARTS.
ONE DAY, I'M GETTING OUT OF HERE...
YEAH— YOU AND EVERYBODY ELSE, AND THEIR UNCLE'S PARA-PARAKEET!
I MEAN IT, RODICE!
FORGET IT, GIRLY. EVEN IF YOU DO GET OUT IT'S NO GOOD...
...'CAUSE NO MATTER HOW FAR YOU GET, THEY'LL FETCH YOU BACK HERE AND BUST YOU TO PIECES.
JUST ASK CLARA PANDY...
NEXT PROG: A LITTLE NIGHT MUSIC.

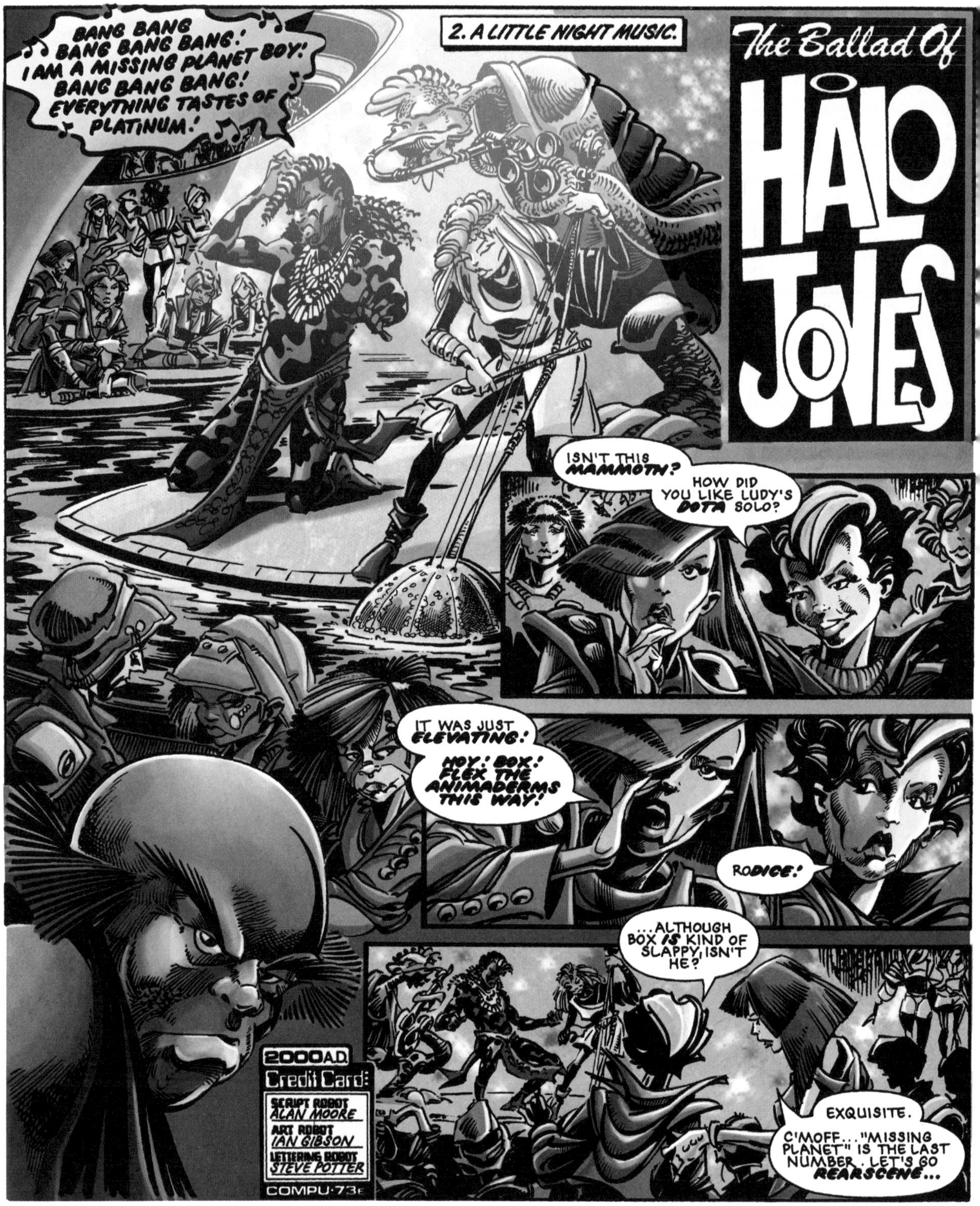

BANG BANG BANG BANG BANG! I AM A MISSING PLANET BOY! BANG BANG BANG! EVERYTHING TASTES OF PLATINUM!
2. A LITTLE NIGHT MUSIC.
The Ballad Of
HALO JONES
ISN'T THIS MAMMOTH?
HOW DID YOU LIKE LUDY'S DOTA SOLO?
IT WAS JUST ELEVATING!
HOY! BOX! FLEX THE ANIMADERMS THIS WAY!
RODICE!
...ALTHOUGH BOX IS KIND OF SLAPPY, ISN'T HE?
EXQUISITE.
C'MOFF... "MISSING PLANET" IS THE LAST NUMBER. LET'S GO REARSCENE...
2000 A.D.
Credit Card:
SCRIPT ROBOT ALAN MOORE
ART ROBOT IAN GIBSON
LETTERING ROBOT STEVE POTTER
COMPU-73E

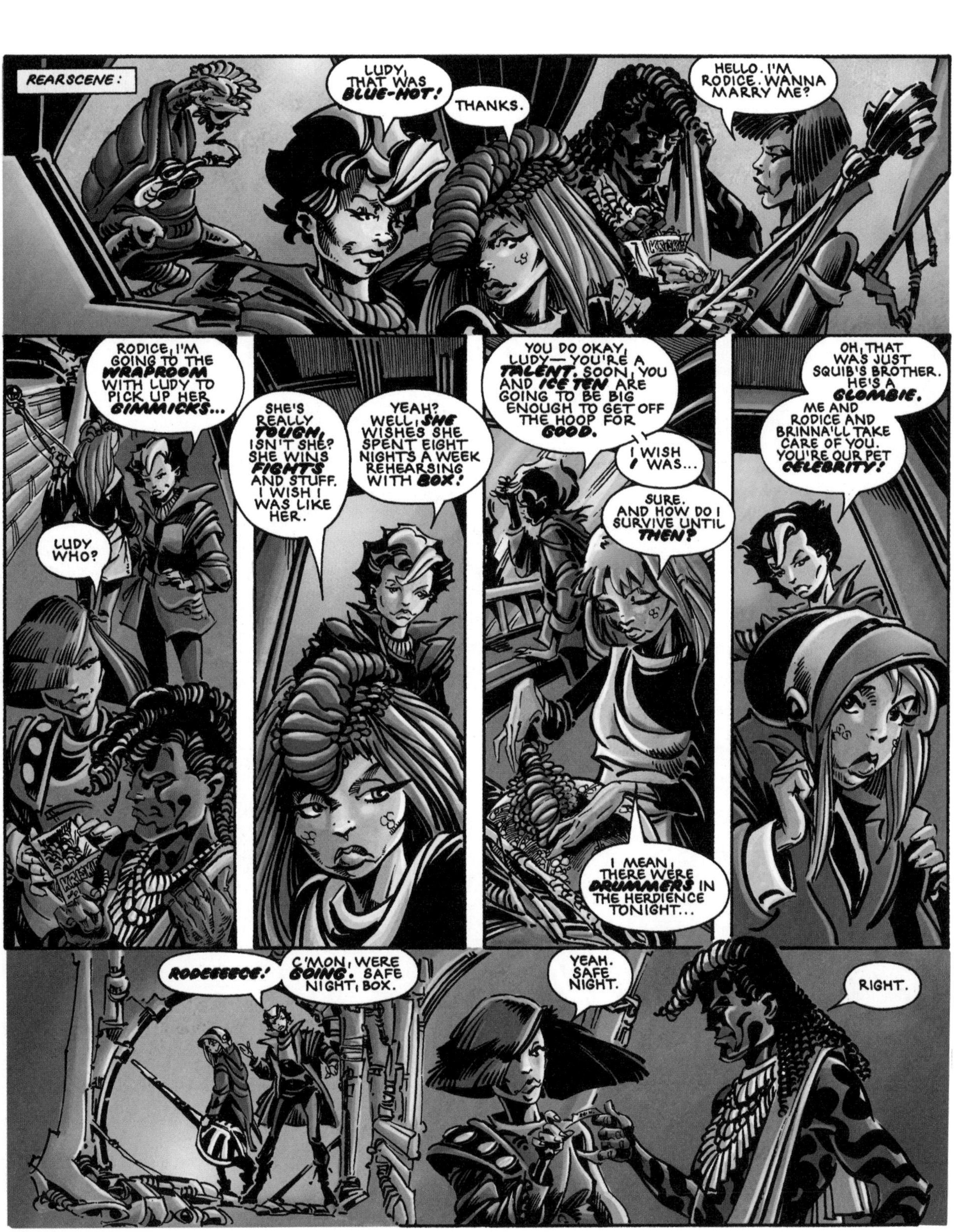
REARSCENE:
LUDY, THAT WAS BLUE-HOT!
THANKS.
HELLO. I'M RODICE. WANNA MARRY ME?
RODICE, I'M GOING TO THE WRAPROOM WITH LUDY TO PICK UP HER GIMMICKS...
LUDY WHO?
SHE'S REALLY TOUGH, ISN'T SHE? SHE WINS FIGHTS AND STUFF. I WISH I WAS LIKE HER.
YEAH? WELL, SHE WISHES SHE SPENT EIGHT NIGHTS A WEEK REHEARSING WITH BOX!
YOU DO OKAY, LUDY— YOU'RE A TALENT. SOON, YOU AND ICE TEN ARE GOING TO BE BIG ENOUGH TO GET OFF THE HOOP FOR GOOD.
I WISH I WAS...
SURE. AND HOW DO I SURVIVE UNTIL THEN?
I MEAN, THERE WERE DRUMMERS IN THE HERDIENCE TONIGHT...
OH, THAT WAS JUST SQUIB'S BROTHER. HE'S A GLOMBIE.
ME AND RODICE AND BRINNA'LL TAKE CARE OF YOU. YOU'RE OUR PET CELEBRITY!
RODEEEECE!
C'MON, WERE GOING. SAFE NIGHT, BOX.
YEAH. SAFE NIGHT.
RIGHT.

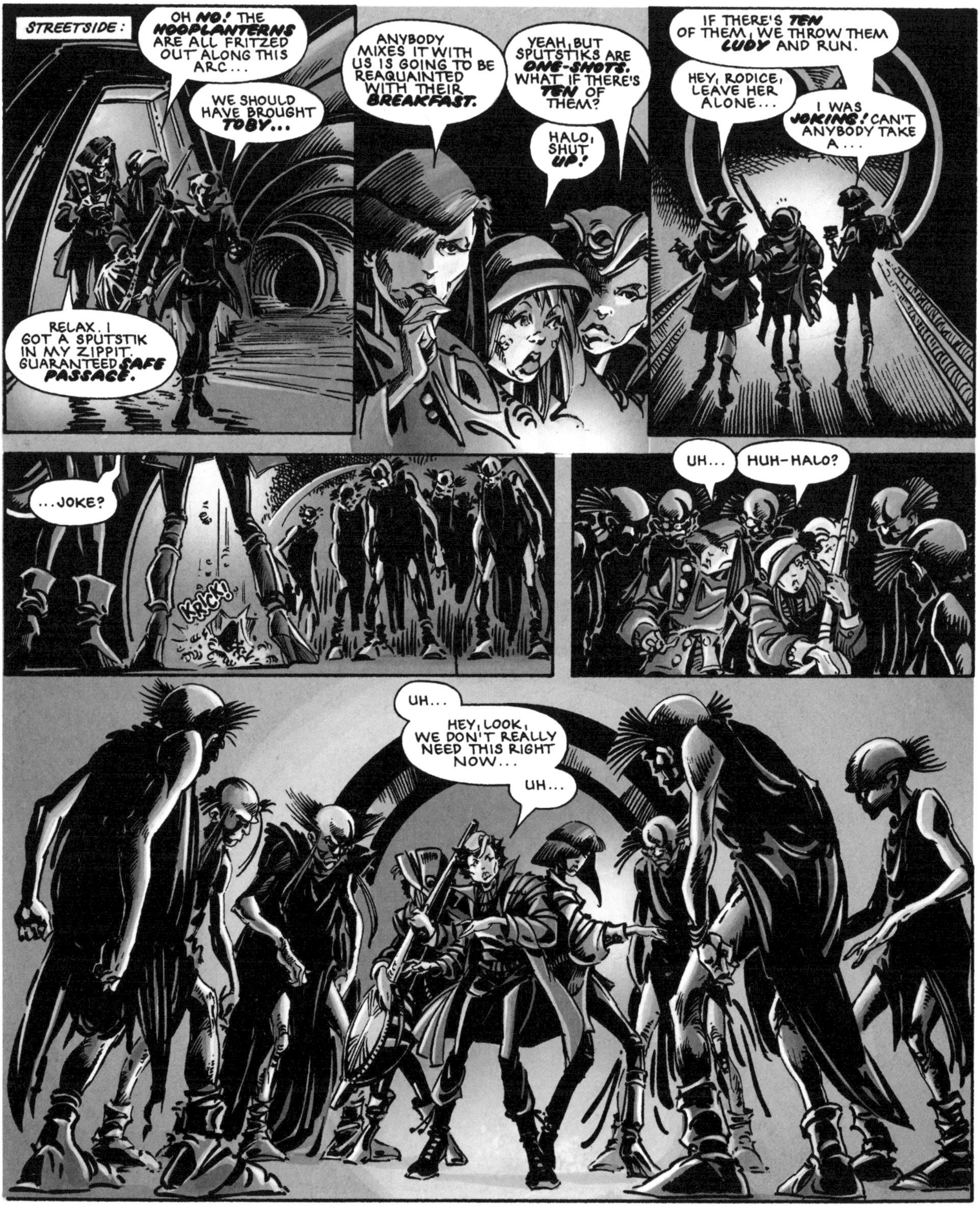
STREETSIDE:
OH NO! THE HOOPLANTERNS ARE ALL FRITZED OUT ALONG THIS ARC...
WE SHOULD HAVE BROUGHT TOBY...
RELAX. I GOT A SPUTSTIK IN MY ZIPPIT. GUARANTEED SAFE PASSAGE.
ANYBODY MIXES IT WITH US IS GOING TO BE REAQUAINTED WITH THEIR BREAKFAST.
YEAH, BUT SPUTSTIKS ARE ONE-SHOTS. WHAT IF THERE'S TEN OF THEM?
HALO, SHUT UP!
IF THERE'S TEN OF THEM, WE THROW THEM LUDY AND RUN.
HEY, RODICE, LEAVE HER ALONE...
I WAS JOKING! CAN'T ANYBODY TAKE A...
...JOKE?
KRICK!
UH...
HUH-HALO?
UH...
HEY, LOOK, WE DON'T REALLY NEED THIS RIGHT NOW...
UH...

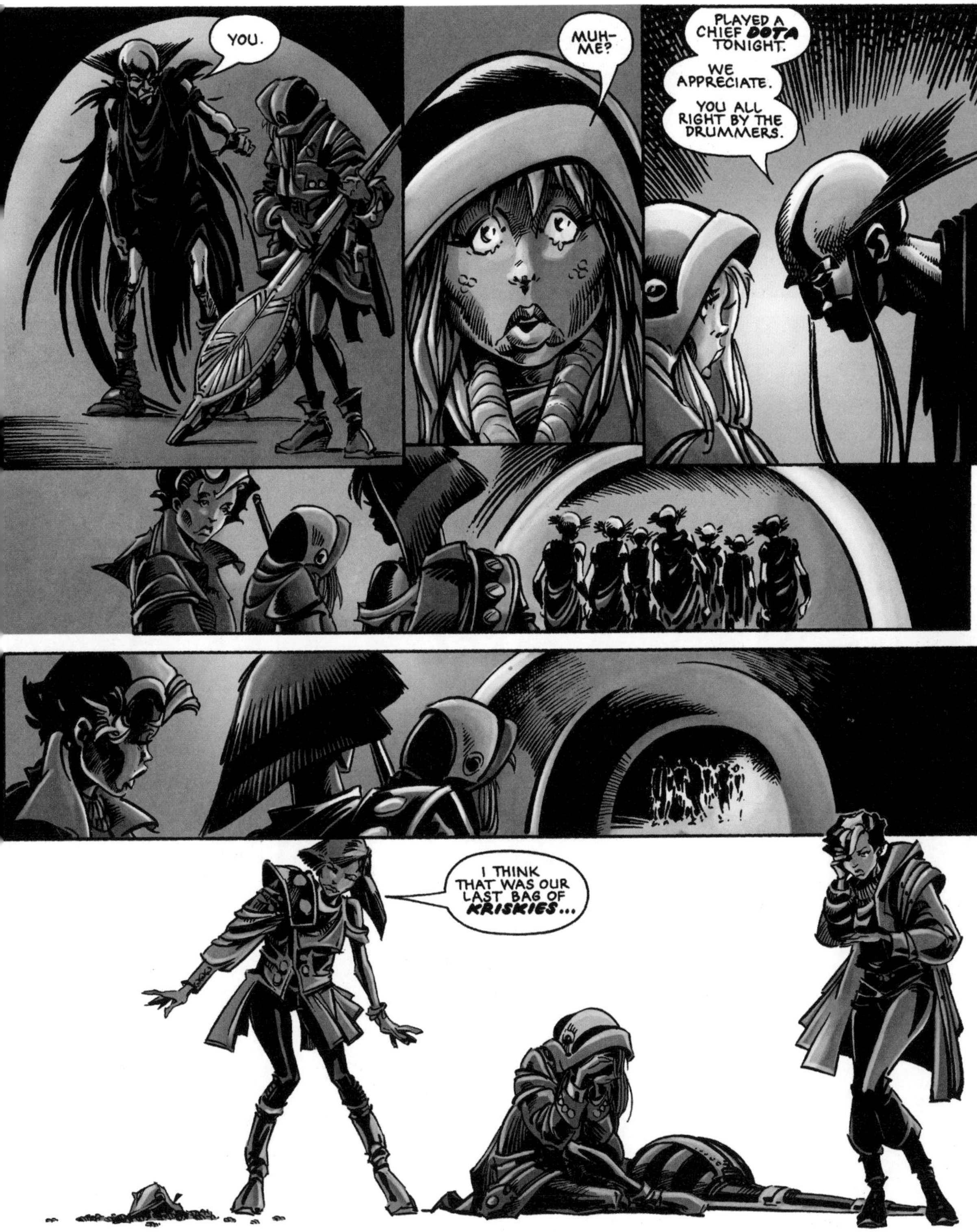
YOU.
MUH-ME?
PLAYED A CHIEF DOTA TONIGHT.
WE APPRECIATE.
YOU ALL RIGHT BY THE DRUMMERS.
I THINK THAT WAS OUR LAST BAG OF KRISKIES...

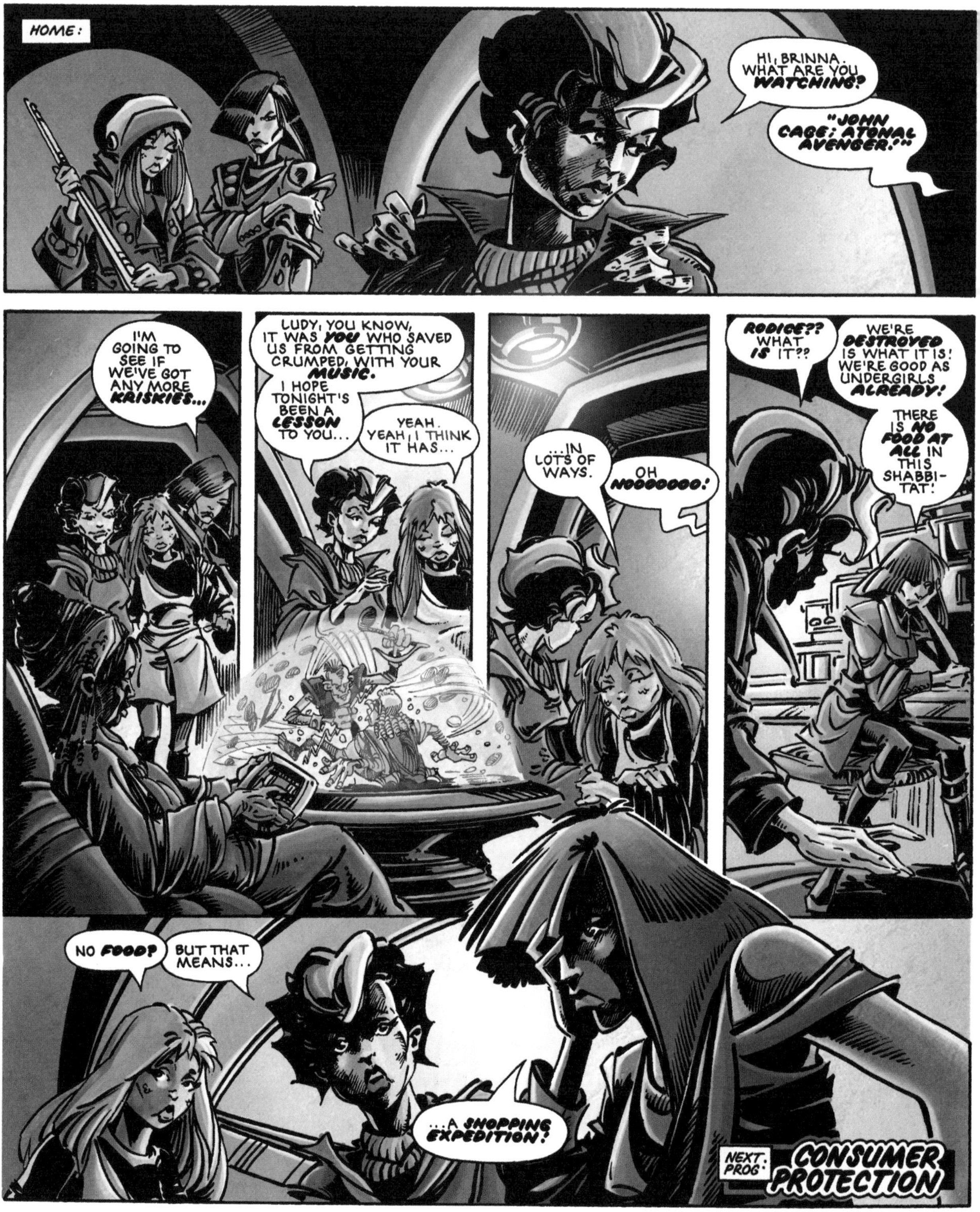
HOME:
HI, BRINNA. WHAT ARE YOU WATCHING?
"JOHN CAGE: ATONAL AVENGER."
I'M GOING TO SEE IF WE'VE GOT ANY MORE KRISKIES...
LUDY, YOU KNOW, IT WAS YOU WHO SAVED US FROM GETTING CRUMPED, WITH YOUR MUSIC.
I HOPE TONIGHT'S BEEN A LESSON TO YOU...
YEAH. YEAH, I THINK IT HAS...
...IN LOTS OF WAYS.
OH NOOOOOOO!
RODICE?? WHAT IS IT??
WE'RE DESTROYED IS WHAT IT IS! WE'RE GOOD AS UNDERGIRLS ALREADY!
THERE IS NO FOOD AT ALL IN THIS SHABBI-TAT!
NO FOOD?
BUT THAT MEANS...
...A SHOPPING EXPEDITION!
NEXT PROG: CONSUMER PROTECTION

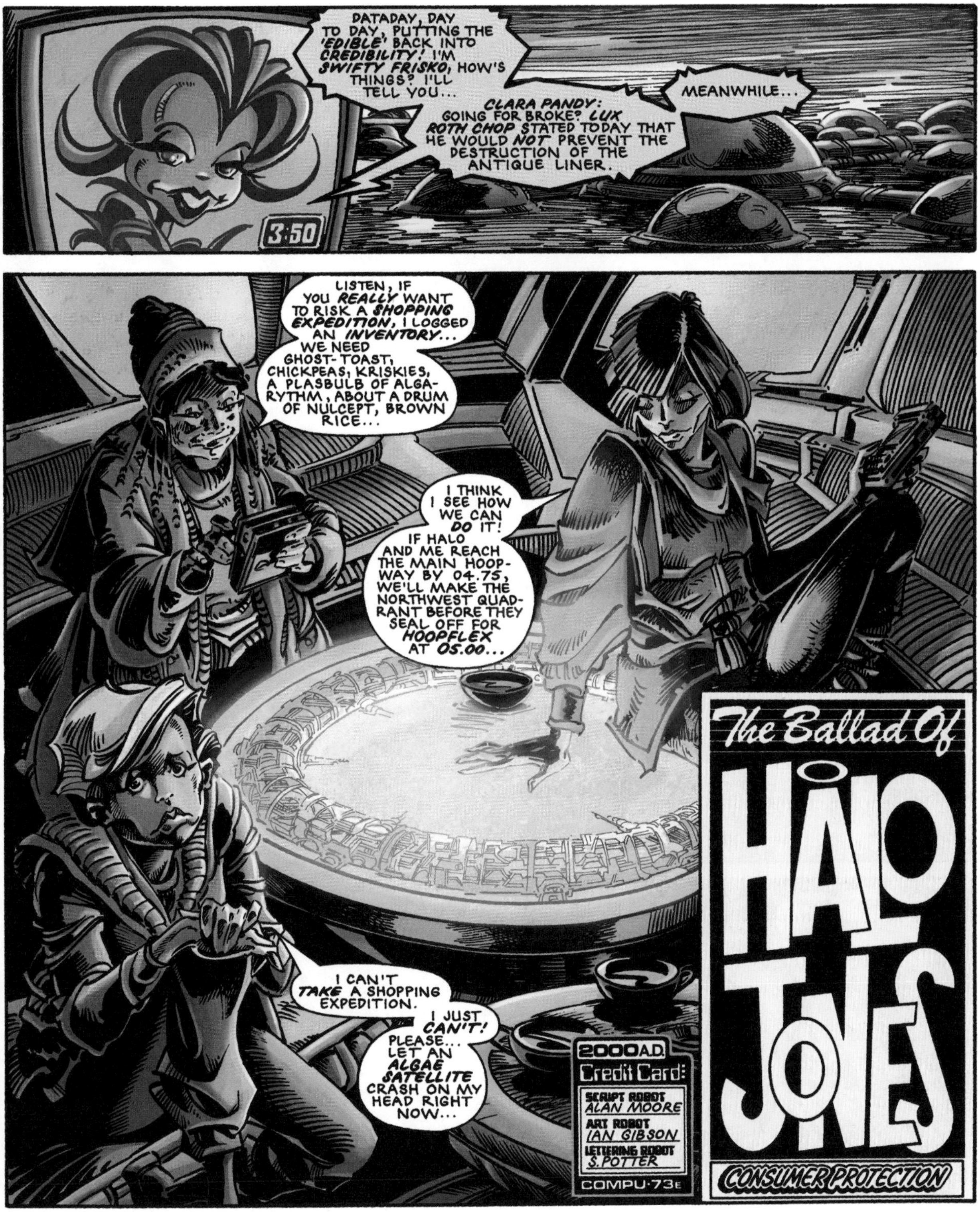
DATADAY, DAY TO DAY, PUTTING THE 'EDIBLE' BACK INTO CREDIBILITY! I'M SWIFTY FRISKO, HOW'S THINGS? I'LL TELL YOU...
CLARA PANDY: GOING FOR BROKE? LUX ROTH CHOP STATED TODAY THAT HE WOULD NOT PREVENT THE DESTRUCTION OF THE ANTIQUE LINER.
MEANWHILE...
3:50
LISTEN, IF YOU REALLY WANT TO RISK A SHOPPING EXPEDITION, I LOGGED AN INVENTORY... WE NEED GHOST-TOAST, CHICKPEAS, KRISKIES, A PLASBULB OF ALGA-RYTHM, ABOUT A DRUM OF NULCEPT, BROWN RICE...
I THINK I SEE HOW WE CAN DO IT! IF HALO AND ME REACH THE MAIN HOOP-WAY BY 04.75, WE'LL MAKE THE NORTHWEST QUAD-RANT BEFORE THEY SEAL OFF FOR HOOPFLEX AT 05.00...
I CAN'T TAKE A SHOPPING EXPEDITION. I JUST CAN'T! PLEASE... LET AN ALGAE SATELLITE CRASH ON MY HEAD RIGHT NOW...
The Ballad Of
HALO JONES
CONSUMER PROTECTION
2000 A.D. Credit Card:
SCRIPT ROBOT ALAN MOORE
ART ROBOT IAN GIBSON
LETTERING ROBOT S.POTTER
COMPU-73E

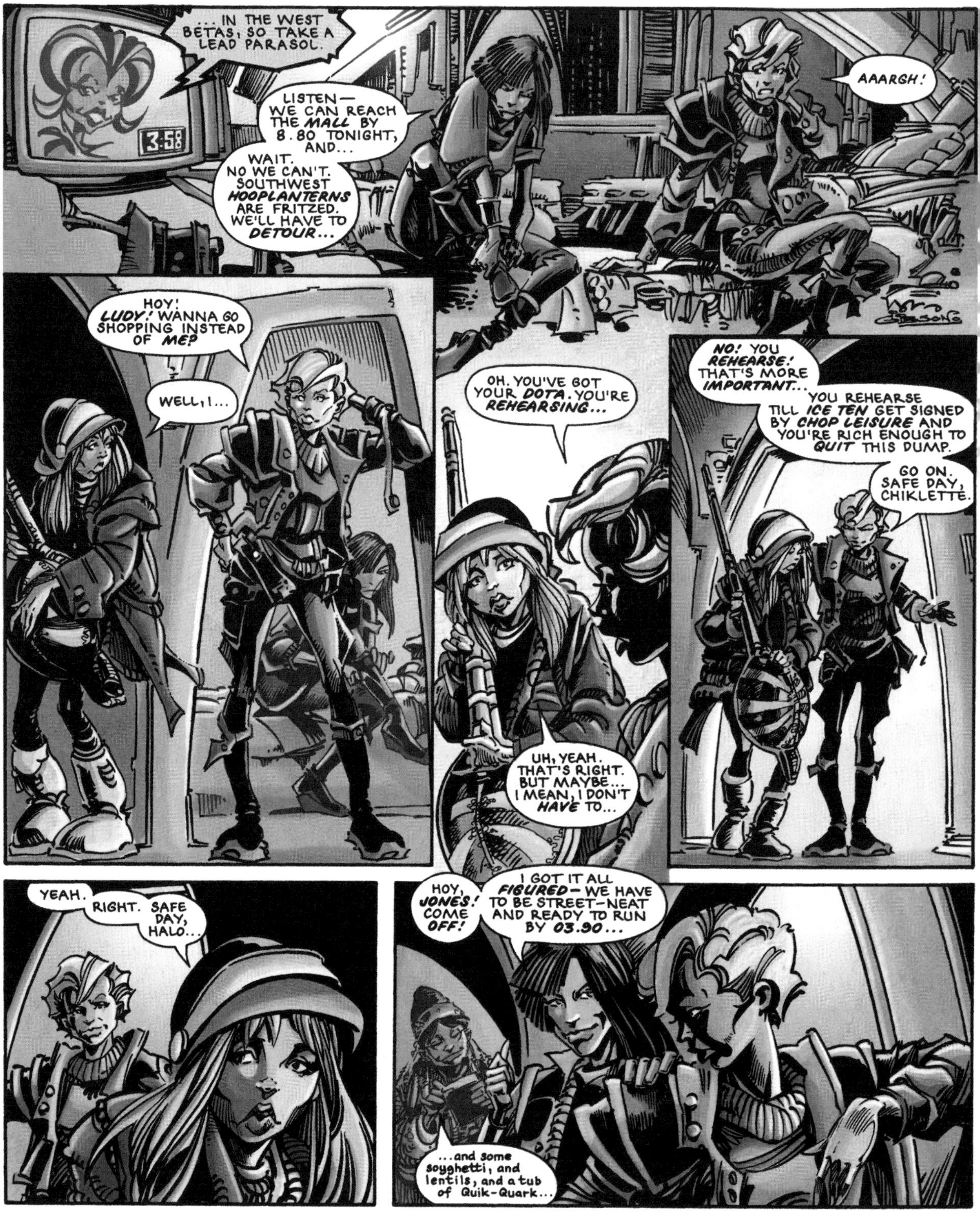

...IN THE WEST BETAS, SO TAKE A LEAD PARASOL.
3:58
LISTEN— WE CAN REACH THE **MALL** BY 8.80 TONIGHT, AND...
WAIT. NO WE CAN'T. SOUTHWEST **HOOPLANTERNS** ARE FRITZED. WE'LL HAVE TO **DETOUR**...
AAARGH!
HOY! **LUDY!** WANNA GO SHOPPING INSTEAD OF **ME?**
WELL, I...
OH. YOU'VE GOT YOUR **DOTA**. YOU'RE **REHEARSING**...
UH, YEAH. THAT'S RIGHT. BUT MAYBE... I MEAN, I DON'T **HAVE** TO...
NO! YOU **REHEARSE!** THAT'S MORE **IMPORTANT**...
YOU REHEARSE TILL **ICE TEN** GET SIGNED BY **CHOP LEISURE** AND YOU'RE RICH ENOUGH TO **QUIT** THIS DUMP.
GO ON. SAFE DAY, CHIKLETTE.
YEAH.
RIGHT. SAFE DAY, HALO...
HOY, **JONES!** COME **OFF!**
I GOT IT ALL **FIGURED**— WE HAVE TO BE STREET-NEAT AND READY TO RUN BY **03.90**...
...and some soyghetti, and lentils, and a tub of Quik-Quark...

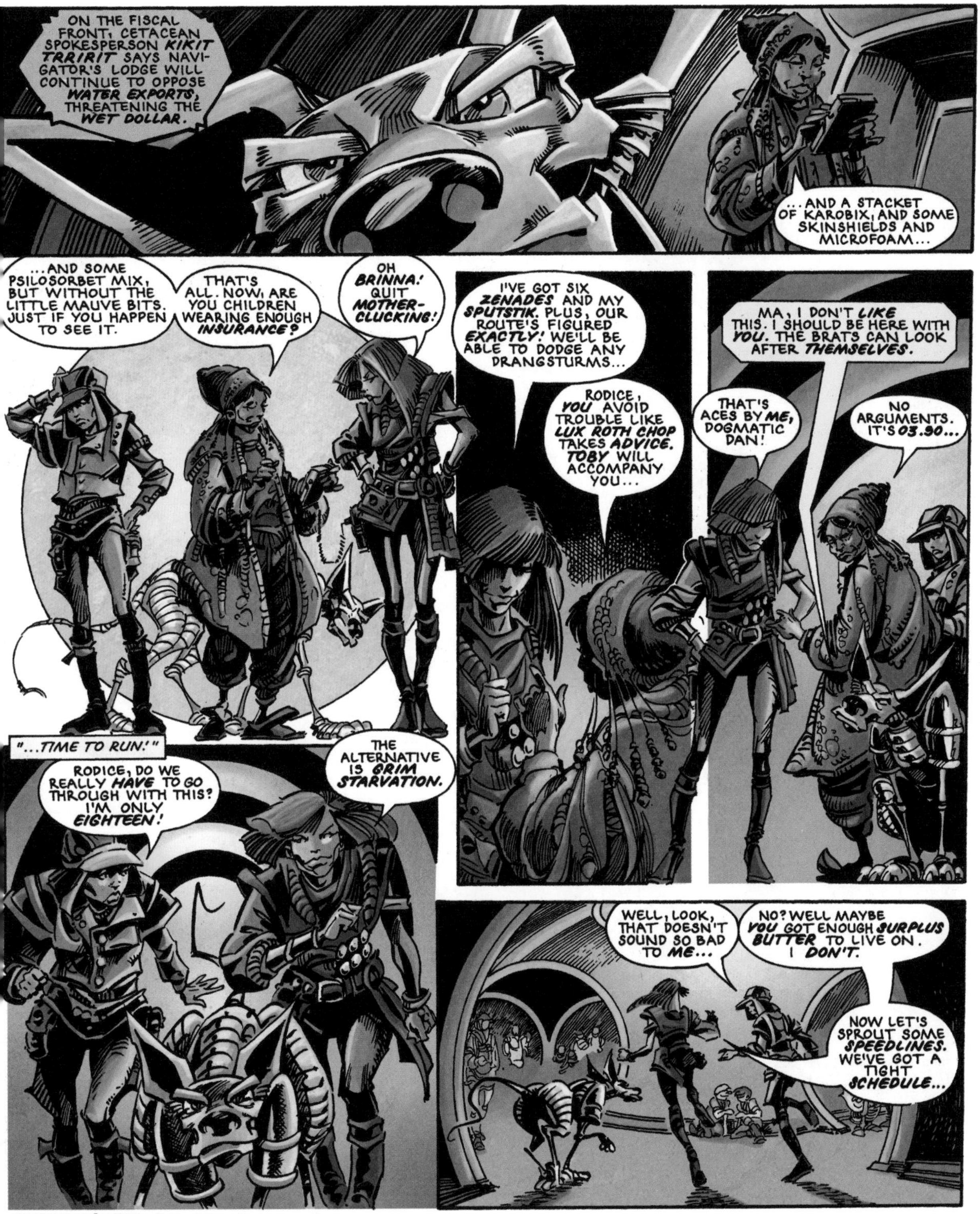
ON THE FISCAL FRONT, CETACEAN SPOKESPERSON KIKIT TRRIRIT SAYS NAVIGATOR'S LODGE WILL CONTINUE TO OPPOSE WATER EXPORTS, THREATENING THE WET DOLLAR.
...AND A STACKET OF KAROBIX, AND SOME SKINSHIELDS AND MICROFOAM...
...AND SOME PSILOSORBET MIX, BUT WITHOUT THE LITTLE MAUVE BITS. JUST IF YOU HAPPEN TO SEE IT.
THAT'S ALL. NOW, ARE YOU CHILDREN WEARING ENOUGH INSURANCE?
OH BRINNA! QUIT MOTHER-CLUCKING!
I'VE GOT SIX ZENADES AND MY SPUTSTIK. PLUS, OUR ROUTE'S FIGURED EXACTLY! WE'LL BE ABLE TO DODGE ANY DRANGSTURMS...
RODICE, YOU AVOID TROUBLE LIKE LUX ROTH CHOP TAKES ADVICE. TOBY WILL ACCOMPANY YOU...
MA, I DON'T LIKE THIS. I SHOULD BE HERE WITH YOU. THE BRATS CAN LOOK AFTER THEMSELVES.
THAT'S ACES BY ME, DOGMATIC DAN!
NO ARGUMENTS. IT'S 03.90...
"...TIME TO RUN!"
RODICE, DO WE REALLY HAVE TO GO THROUGH WITH THIS? I'M ONLY EIGHTEEN!
THE ALTERNATIVE IS GRIM STARVATION.
WELL, LOOK, THAT DOESN'T SOUND SO BAD TO ME...
NO? WELL MAYBE YOU GOT ENOUGH SURPLUS BUTTER TO LIVE ON. I DON'T.
NOW LET'S SPROUT SOME SPEEDLINES. WE'VE GOT A TIGHT SCHEDULE...

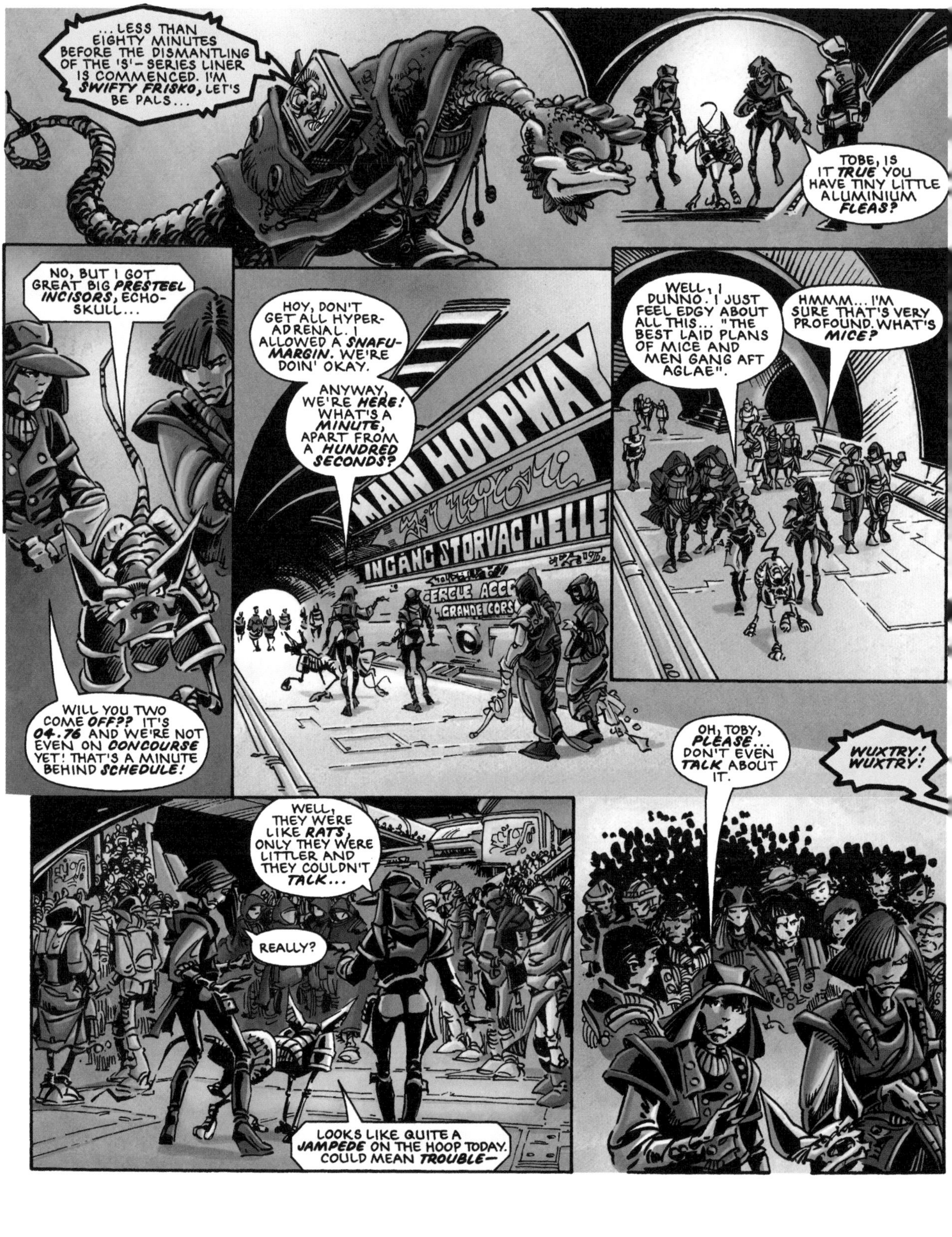

...LESS THAN EIGHTY MINUTES BEFORE THE DISMANTLING OF THE 'S'-SERIES LINER IS COMMENCED. I'M SWIFTY FRISKO, LET'S BE PALS...
TOBE, IS IT TRUE YOU HAVE TINY LITTLE ALUMINIUM FLEAS?
NO, BUT I GOT GREAT BIG PRESTEEL INCISORS, ECHO-SKULL...
WILL YOU TWO COME OFF?? IT'S 04.76 AND WE'RE NOT EVEN ON CONCOURSE YET! THAT'S A MINUTE BEHIND SCHEDULE!
HOY, DON'T GET ALL HYPER-ADRENAL. I ALLOWED A SNAFU-MARGIN. WE'RE DOIN' OKAY.
ANYWAY, WE'RE HERE! WHAT'S A MINUTE, APART FROM A HUNDRED SECONDS?
MAIN HOOPWAY
INGANG STORVAG MELLE
CERCLE ACC
GRANDE CORS
WELL, I DUNNO. I JUST FEEL EDGY ABOUT ALL THIS... "THE BEST LAID PLANS OF MICE AND MEN GANG AFT AGLAE".
HMMM... I'M SURE THAT'S VERY PROFOUND. WHAT'S MICE?
WELL, THEY WERE LIKE RATS, ONLY THEY WERE LITTLER AND THEY COULDN'T TALK...
REALLY?
LOOKS LIKE QUITE A JAMPEDE ON THE HOOP TODAY. COULD MEAN TROUBLE—
OH, TOBY, PLEASE... DON'T EVEN TALK ABOUT IT.
WUXTRY! WUXTRY!

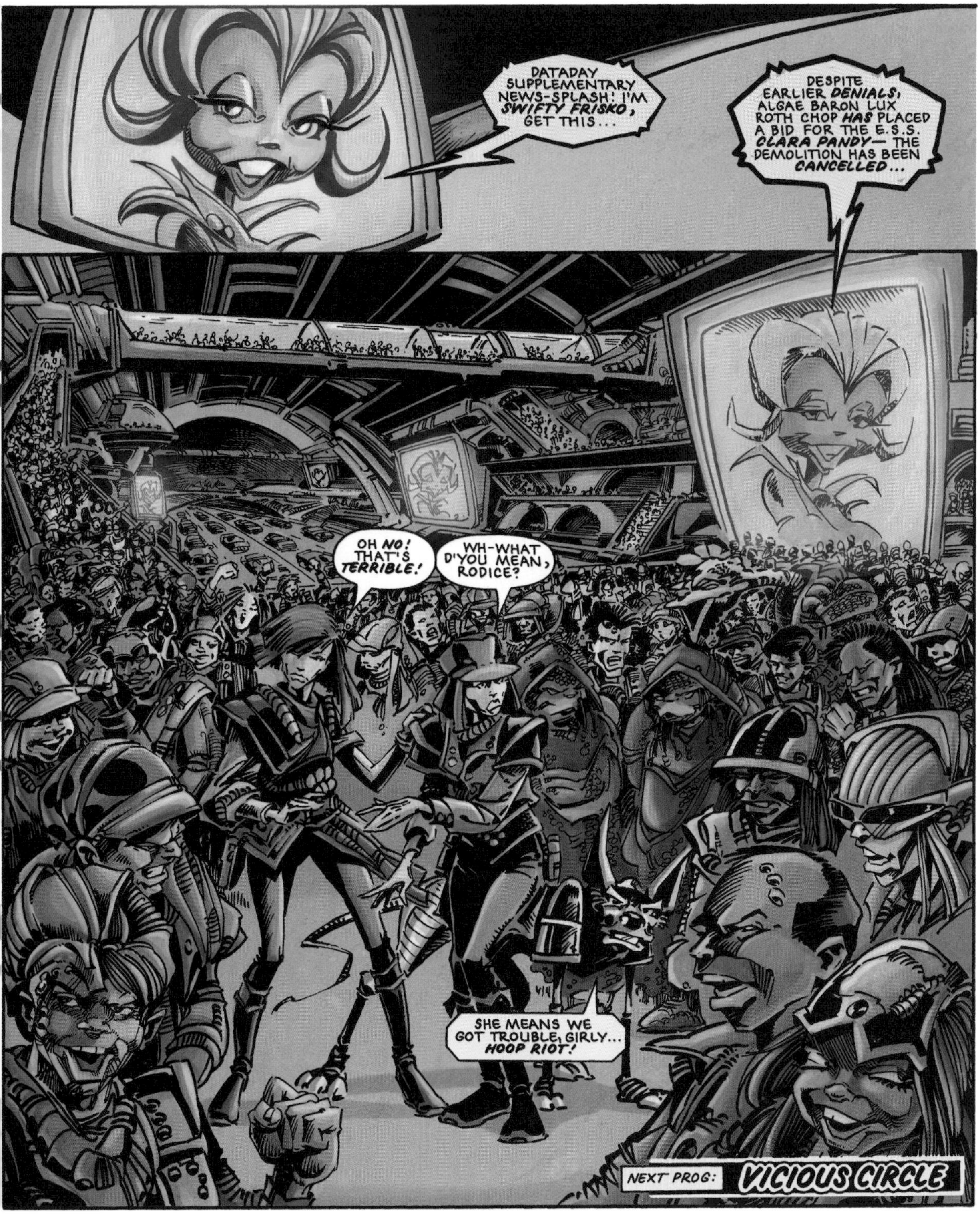
DATADAY SUPPLEMENTARY NEWS-SPLASH! I'M SWIFTY FRISKO, GET THIS...
DESPITE EARLIER DENIALS, ALGAE BARON LUX ROTH CHOP HAS PLACED A BID FOR THE E.S.S. CLARA PANDY— THE DEMOLITION HAS BEEN CANCELLED...
OH NO! THAT'S TERRIBLE!
WH-WHAT D'YOU MEAN, RODICE?
SHE MEANS WE GOT TROUBLE, GIRLY... HOOP RIOT!
NEXT PROG: VICIOUS CIRCLE

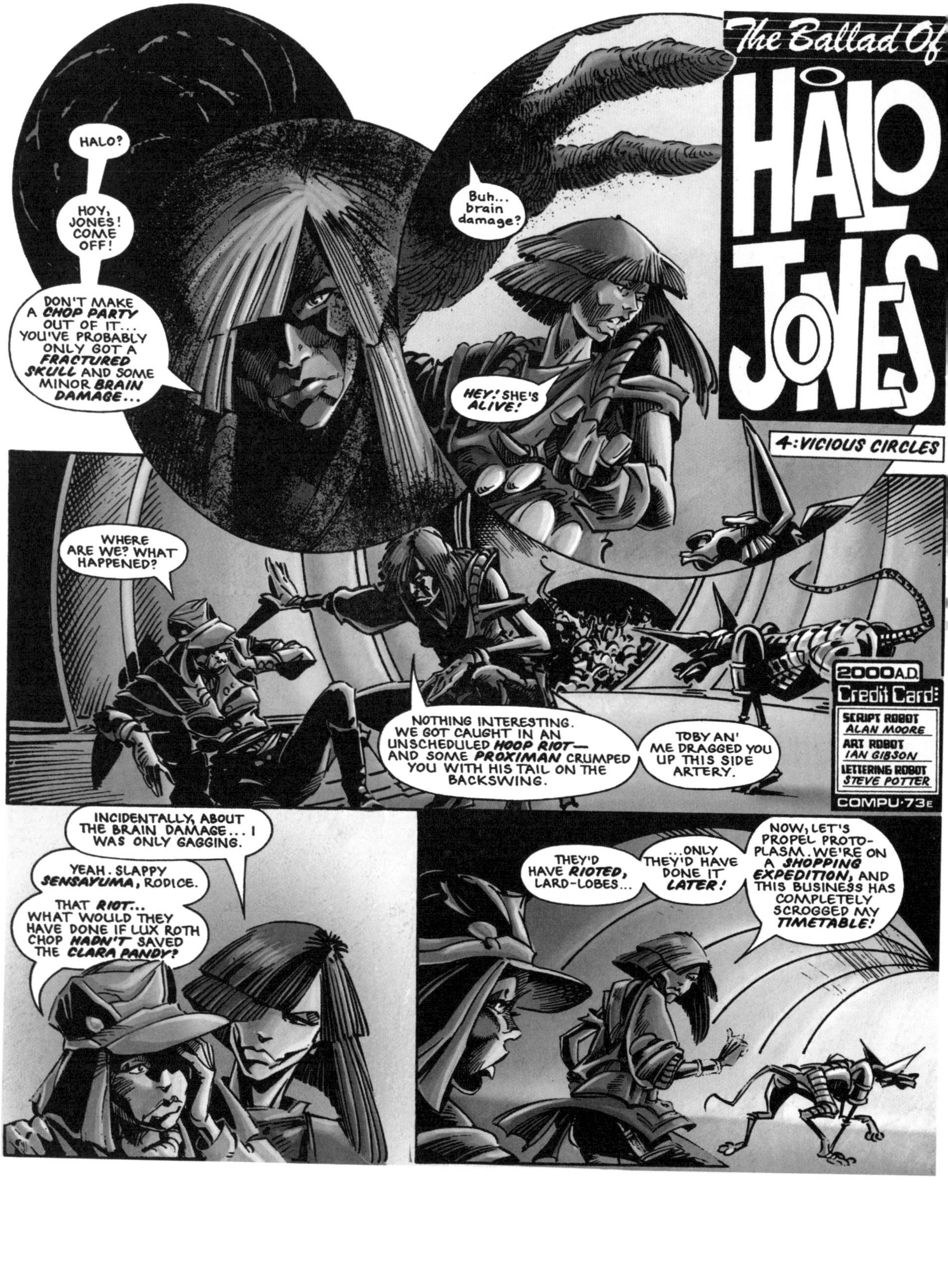

The Ballad Of
HALO JONES
4: VICIOUS CIRCLES
HALO?
HOY, JONES! COME OFF!
DON'T MAKE A CHOP PARTY OUT OF IT... YOU'VE PROBABLY ONLY GOT A FRACTURED SKULL AND SOME MINOR BRAIN DAMAGE...
Buh... brain damage?
HEY! SHE'S ALIVE!
WHERE ARE WE? WHAT HAPPENED?
NOTHING INTERESTING. WE GOT CAUGHT IN AN UNSCHEDULED HOOP RIOT— AND SOME PROXIMAN CRUMPED YOU WITH HIS TAIL ON THE BACKSWING.
TOBY AN' ME DRAGGED YOU UP THIS SIDE ARTERY.
2000 A.D.
Credit Card:
SCRIPT ROBOT ALAN MOORE
ART ROBOT IAN GIBSON
LETTERING ROBOT STEVE POTTER
COMPU·73E
INCIDENTALLY, ABOUT THE BRAIN DAMAGE... I WAS ONLY GAGGING.
YEAH. SLAPPY SENSAYUMA, RODICE.
THAT RIOT... WHAT WOULD THEY HAVE DONE IF LUX ROTH CHOP HADN'T SAVED THE CLARA PANDY?
THEY'D HAVE RIOTED, LARD-LOBES...
...ONLY THEY'D HAVE DONE IT LATER!
NOW, LET'S PROPEL PROTO-PLASM. WE'RE ON A SHOPPING EXPEDITION, AND THIS BUSINESS HAS COMPLETELY SCROGGED MY TIMETABLE!

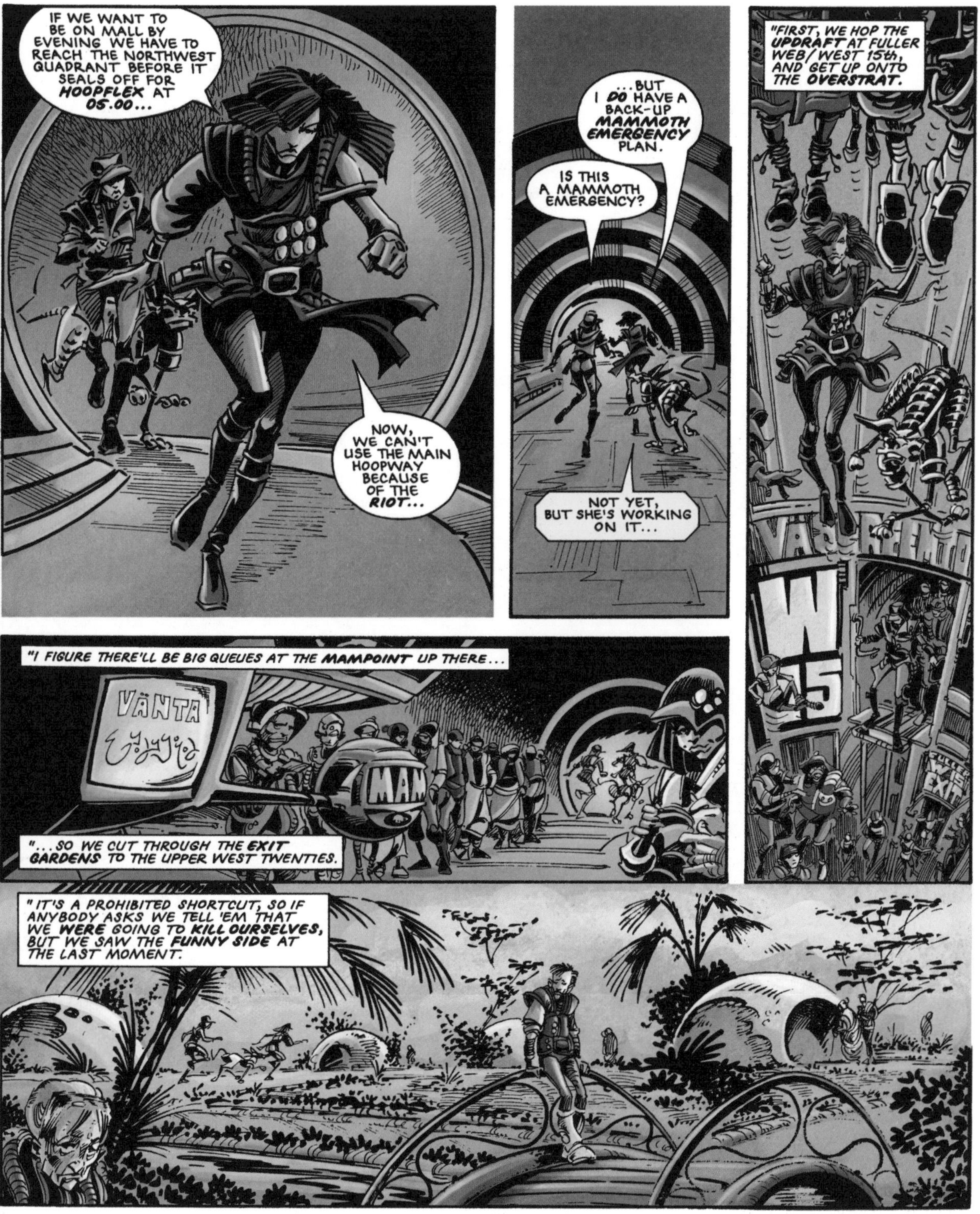
IF WE WANT TO BE ON MALL BY EVENING WE HAVE TO REACH THE NORTHWEST QUADRANT BEFORE IT SEALS OFF FOR HOOPFLEX AT 05.00...
NOW, WE CAN'T USE THE MAIN HOOPWAY BECAUSE OF THE RIOT...
...BUT I DO HAVE A BACK-UP MAMMOTH EMERGENCY PLAN.
IS THIS A MAMMOTH EMERGENCY?
NOT YET, BUT SHE'S WORKING ON IT...
"FIRST, WE HOP THE UPDRAFT AT FULLER WEB/WEST 15th, AND GET UP ONTO THE OVERSTRAT.
W
15
"I FIGURE THERE'LL BE BIG QUEUES AT THE MAMPOINT UP THERE...
VÄNTA
MAM
"...SO WE CUT THROUGH THE EXIT GARDENS TO THE UPPER WEST TWENTIES.
"IT'S A PROHIBITED SHORTCUT, SO IF ANYBODY ASKS WE TELL 'EM THAT WE WERE GOING TO KILL OURSELVES, BUT WE SAW THE FUNNY SIDE AT THE LAST MOMENT.

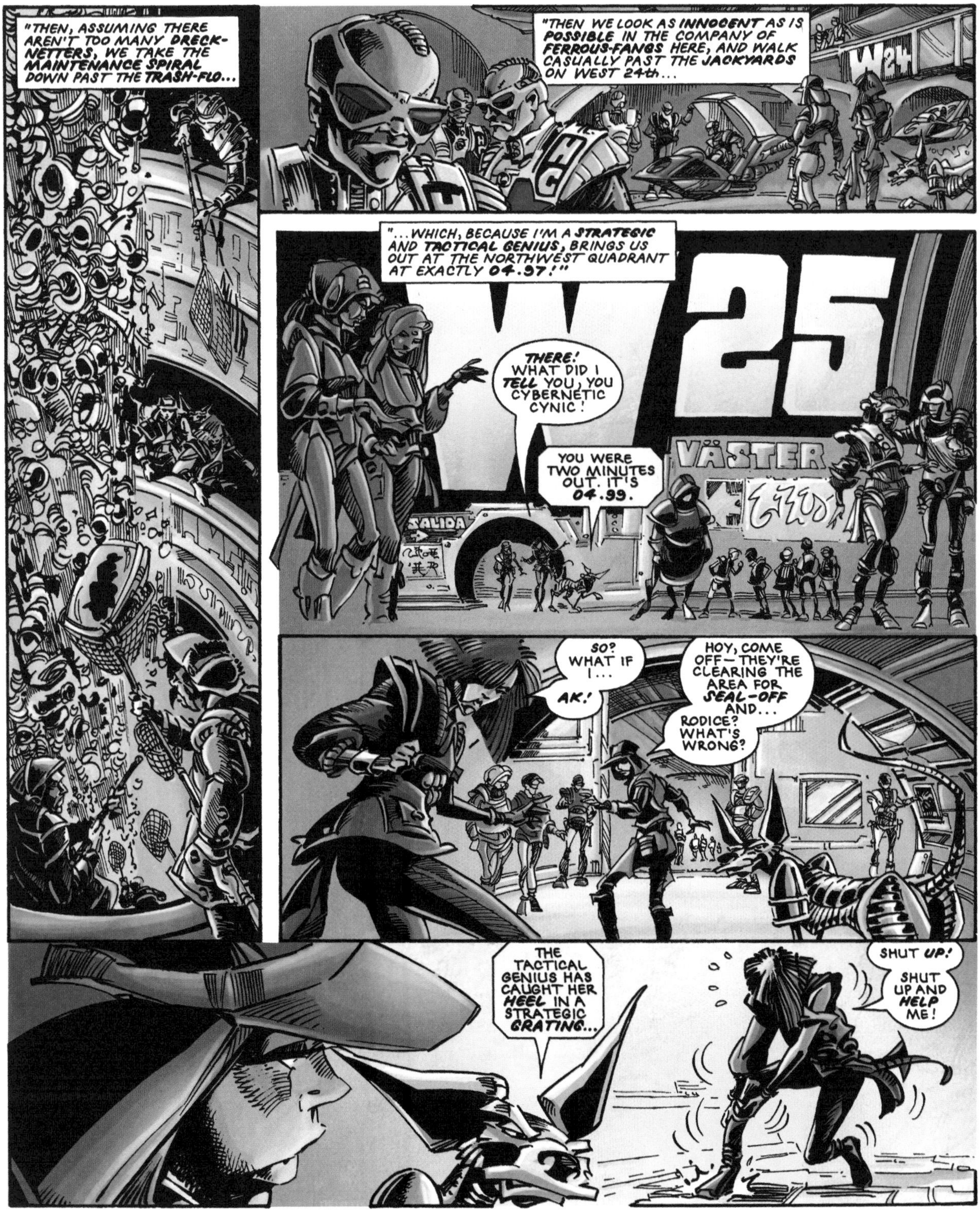
"THEN, ASSUMING THERE AREN'T TOO MANY DRECK-NETTERS, WE TAKE THE MAINTENANCE SPIRAL DOWN PAST THE TRASH-FLO...
"THEN WE LOOK AS INNOCENT AS IS POSSIBLE IN THE COMPANY OF FERROUS-FANGS HERE, AND WALK CASUALLY PAST THE JACKYARDS ON WEST 24th...
W24
"...WHICH, BECAUSE I'M A STRATEGIC AND TACTICAL GENIUS, BRINGS US OUT AT THE NORTHWEST QUADRANT AT EXACTLY 04.97!"
W25
THERE! WHAT DID I TELL YOU, YOU CYBERNETIC CYNIC!
YOU WERE TWO MINUTES OUT. IT'S 04.99.
VÄSTER
SALIDA
SO? WHAT IF I...
AK!
HOY, COME OFF— THEY'RE CLEARING THE AREA FOR SEAL-OFF AND...
RODICE? WHAT'S WRONG?
THE TACTICAL GENIUS HAS CAUGHT HER HEEL IN A STRATEGIC GRATING...
SHUT UP!
SHUT UP AND HELP ME!

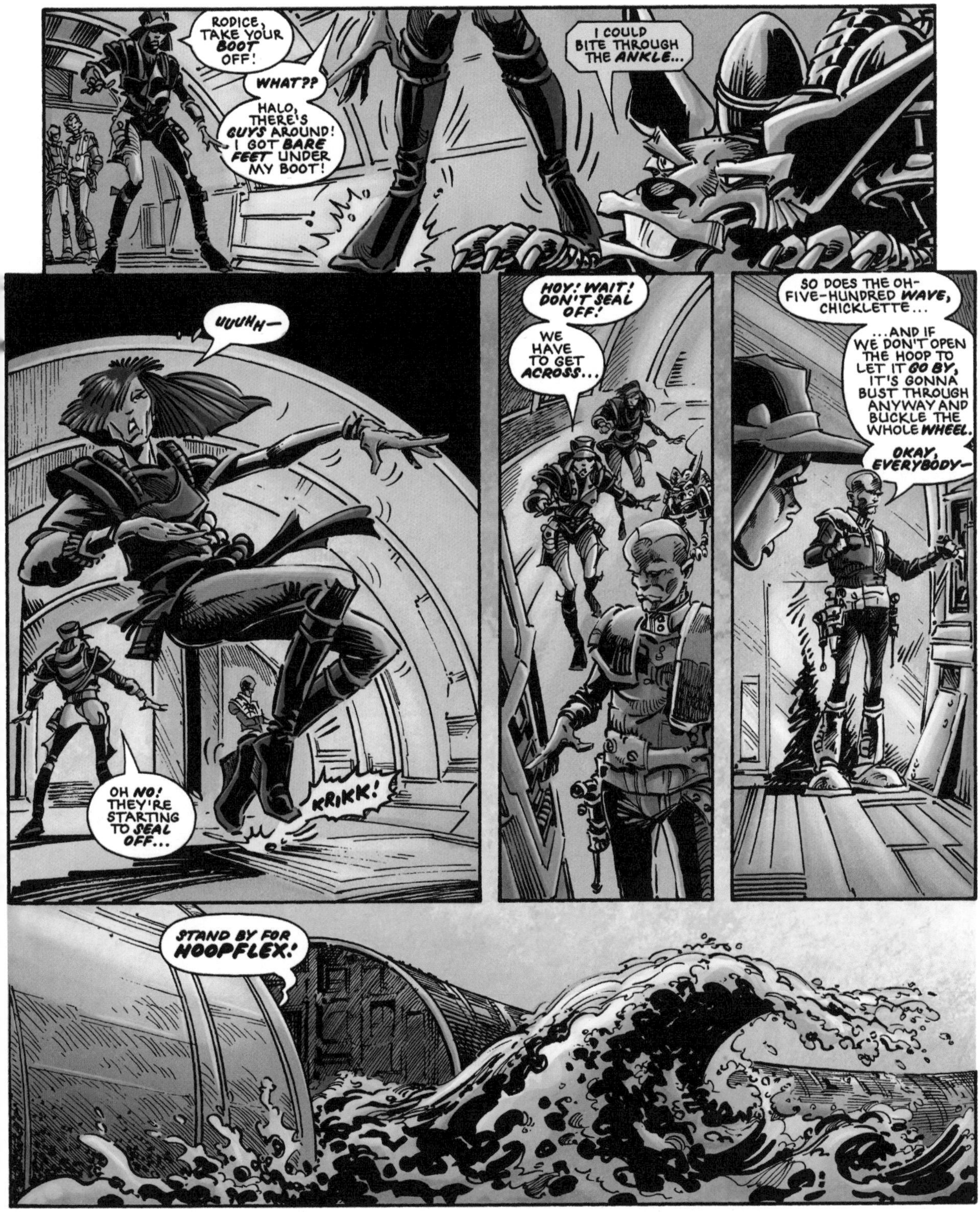

RODICE, TAKE YOUR BOOT OFF!
WHAT??
HALO, THERE'S GUYS AROUND! I GOT BARE FEET UNDER MY BOOT!
I COULD BITE THROUGH THE ANKLE...
UUUHH—
OH NO! THEY'RE STARTING TO SEAL OFF...
KRIKK!
HOY! WAIT! DON'T SEAL OFF!
WE HAVE TO GET ACROSS...
SO DOES THE OH-FIVE-HUNDRED WAVE, CHICKLETTE...
...AND IF WE DON'T OPEN THE HOOP TO LET IT GO BY, IT'S GONNA BUST THROUGH ANYWAY AND BUCKLE THE WHOLE WHEEL.
OKAY, EVERYBODY—
STAND BY FOR HOOPFLEX!

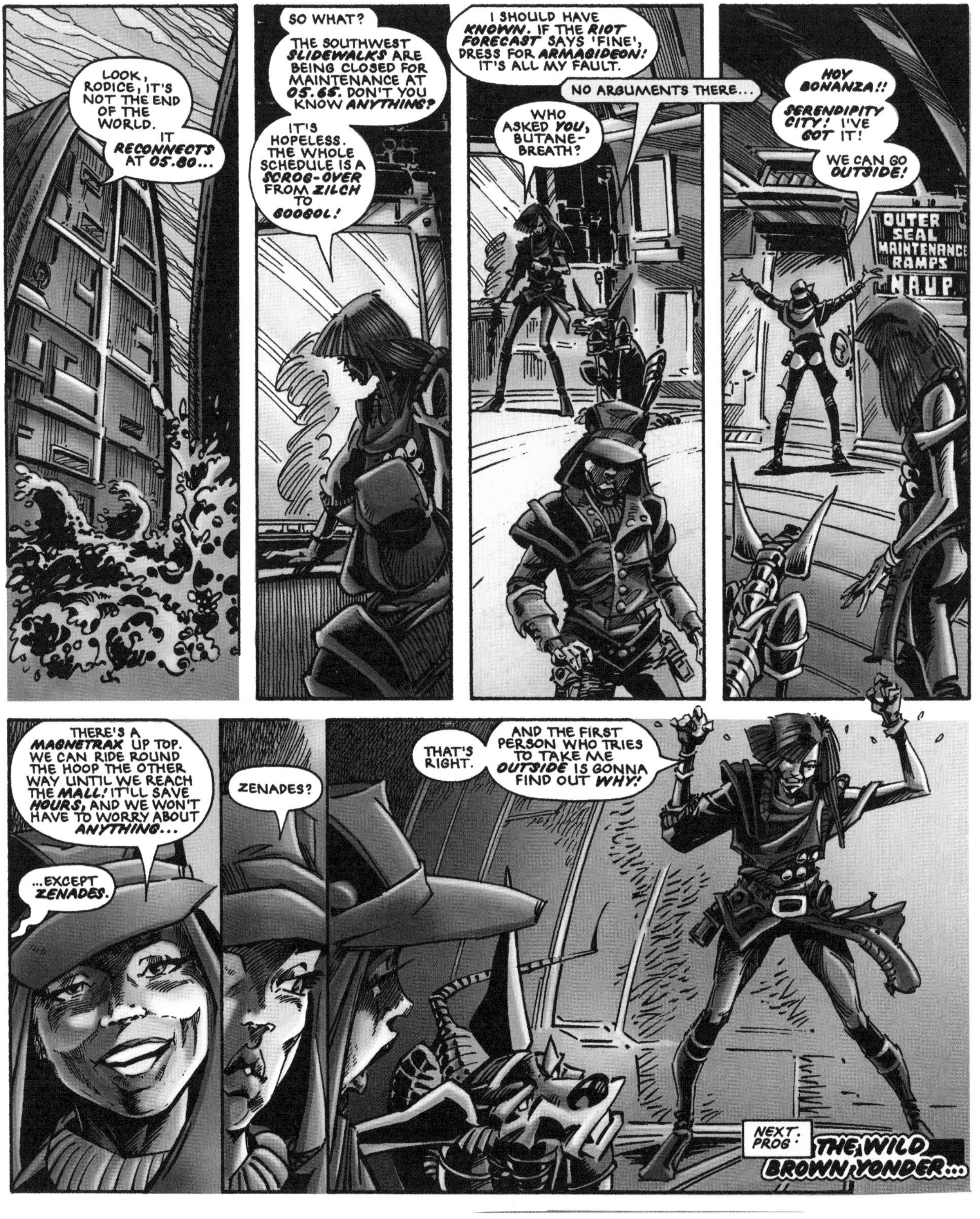

LOOK, RODICE, IT'S NOT THE END OF THE WORLD.
IT RECONNECTS AT 05.80...
SO WHAT?
THE SOUTHWEST SLIDEWALKS ARE BEING CLOSED FOR MAINTENANCE AT 05.65. DON'T YOU KNOW ANYTHING?
IT'S HOPELESS. THE WHOLE SCHEDULE IS A SCROG-OVER FROM ZILCH TO GOOGOL!
I SHOULD HAVE KNOWN. IF THE RIOT FORECAST SAYS 'FINE', DRESS FOR ARMAGIDEON! IT'S ALL MY FAULT.
NO ARGUMENTS THERE...
WHO ASKED YOU, BUTANE-BREATH?
HOY BONANZA!!
SERENDIPITY CITY! I'VE GOT IT!
WE CAN GO OUTSIDE!
OUTER SEAL MAINTENANCE RAMPS
N.A.U.P.
THERE'S A MAGNETRAX UP TOP. WE CAN RIDE ROUND THE HOOP THE OTHER WAY UNTIL WE REACH THE MALL! IT'LL SAVE HOURS, AND WE WON'T HAVE TO WORRY ABOUT ANYTHING...
...EXCEPT ZENADES.
ZENADES?
THAT'S RIGHT.
AND THE FIRST PERSON WHO TRIES TO TAKE ME OUTSIDE IS GONNA FIND OUT WHY!
NEXT PROG: THE WILD BROWN YONDER...

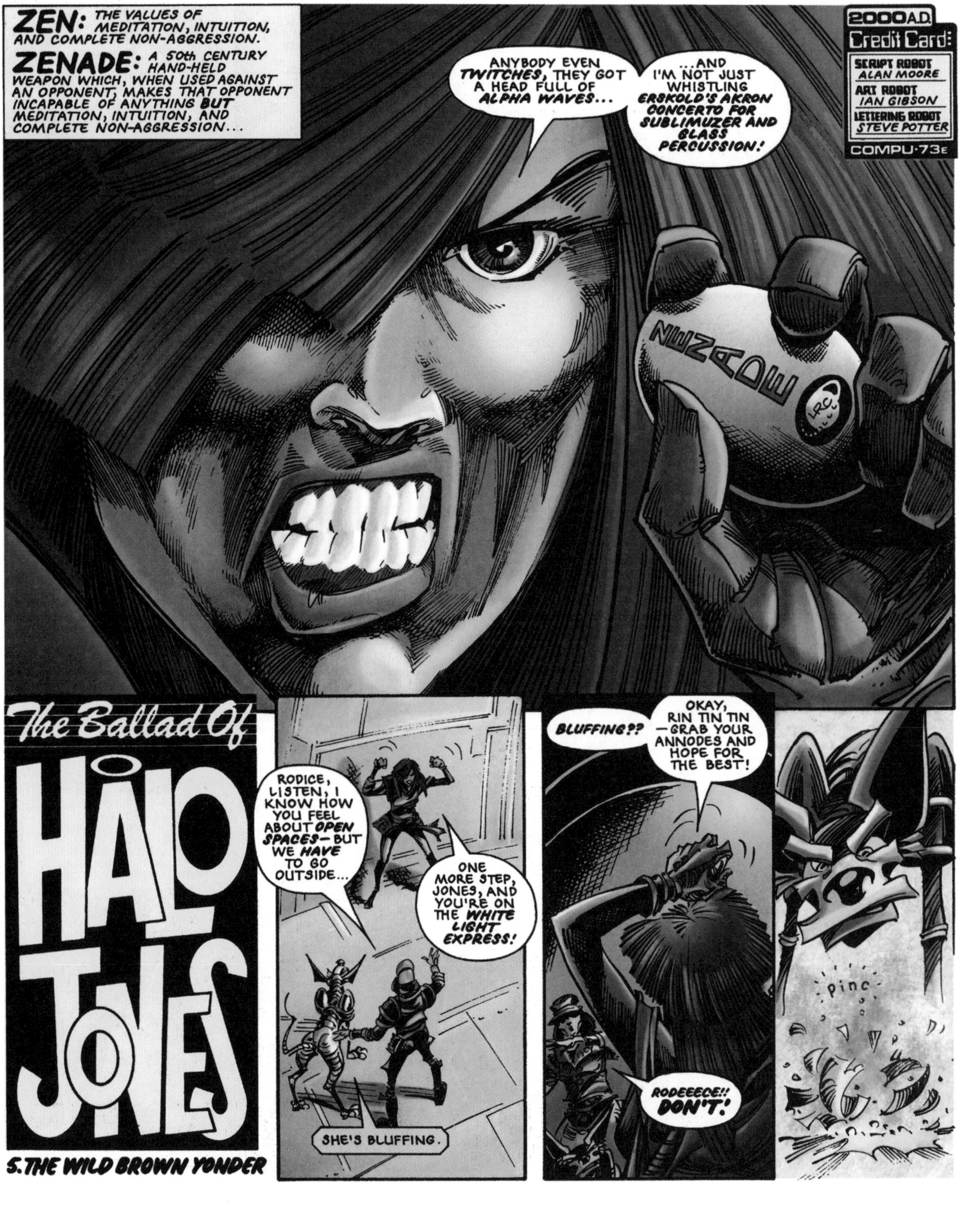
ZEN: THE VALUES OF MEDITATION, INTUITION, AND COMPLETE NON-AGGRESSION.
ZENADE: A 50th CENTURY HAND-HELD WEAPON WHICH, WHEN USED AGAINST AN OPPONENT, MAKES THAT OPPONENT INCAPABLE OF ANYTHING BUT MEDITATION, INTUITION, AND COMPLETE NON-AGGRESSION...
2000 A.D. Credit Card: SCRIPT ROBOT ALAN MOORE ART ROBOT IAN GIBSON LETTERING ROBOT STEVE POTTER COMPU·73E
ANYBODY EVEN TWITCHES, THEY GOT A HEAD FULL OF ALPHA WAVES...
...AND I'M NOT JUST WHISTLING ERSKOLD'S AKRON CONCERTO FOR SUBLIMUZER AND GLASS PERCUSSION!
NEWZADE
The Ballad Of
HALO JONES
5. THE WILD BROWN YONDER
RODICE, LISTEN, I KNOW HOW YOU FEEL ABOUT OPEN SPACES— BUT WE HAVE TO GO OUTSIDE...
ONE MORE STEP, JONES, AND YOU'RE ON THE WHITE LIGHT EXPRESS!
SHE'S BLUFFING.
BLUFFING??
OKAY, RIN TIN TIN —GRAB YOUR ANNODES AND HOPE FOR THE BEST!
RODEEECE!! DON'T!
pinc

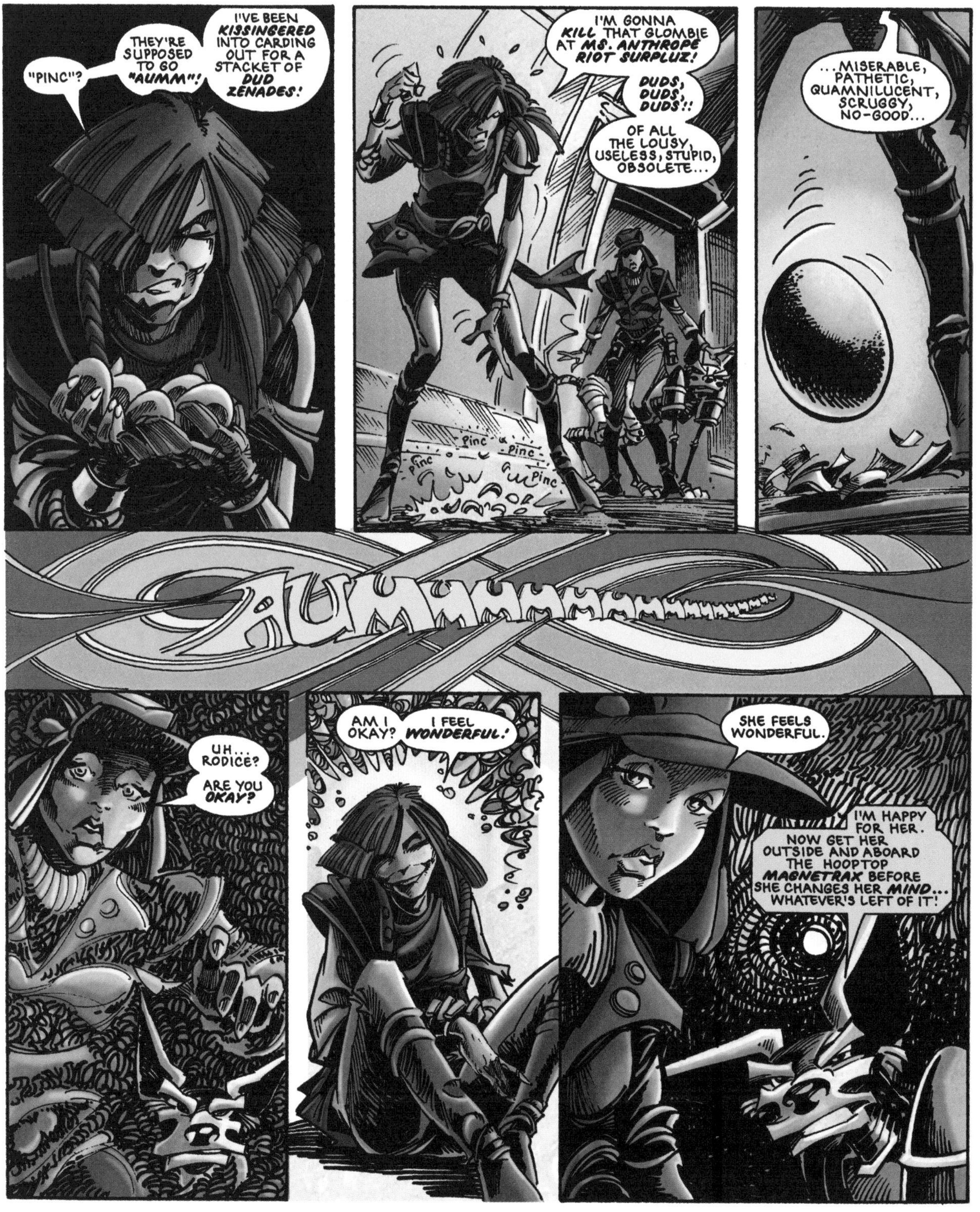

"PINC"?
THEY'RE SUPPOSED TO GO "AUMM"!
I'VE BEEN KISSINGERED INTO CARDING OUT FOR A STACKET OF DUD ZENADES!
I'M GONNA KILL THAT GLOMBIE AT MS. ANTHROPE RIOT SURPLUZ!
DUDS, DUDS, DUDS!!
OF ALL THE LOUSY, USELESS, STUPID, OBSOLETE...
Pinc Pinc Pinc Pinc Pinc
...MISERABLE, PATHETIC, QUAMNILUCENT, SCRUGGY, NO-GOOD...
AUMMMMMMMMMMMMMMMM
UH... RODICE?
ARE YOU OKAY?
AM I OKAY?
I FEEL WONDERFUL!
SHE FEELS WONDERFUL.
I'M HAPPY FOR HER. NOW GET HER OUTSIDE AND ABOARD THE HOOPTOP MAGNETRAX BEFORE SHE CHANGES HER MIND... WHATEVER'S LEFT OF IT!

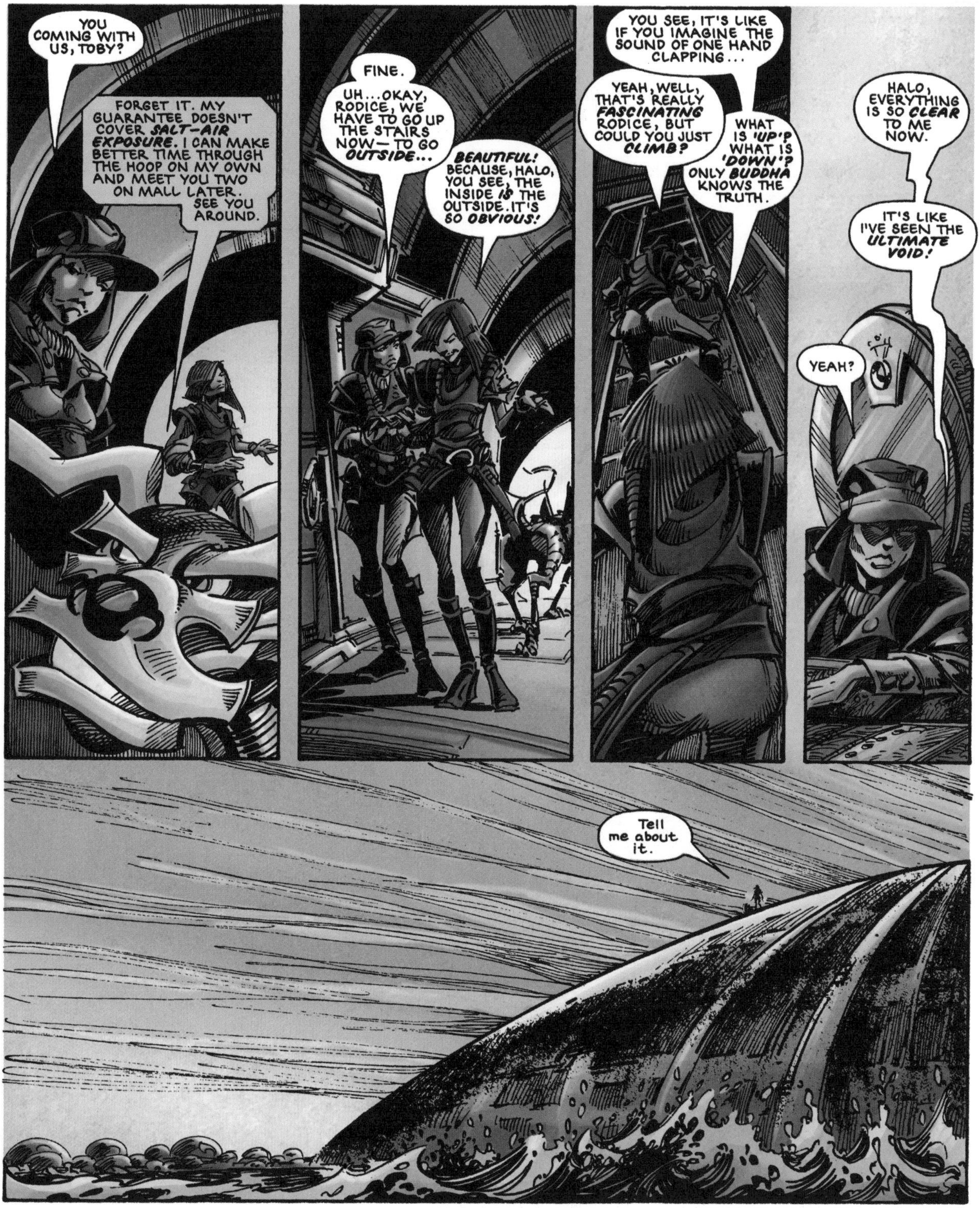

YOU COMING WITH US, TOBY?
FORGET IT. MY GUARANTEE DOESN'T COVER SALT-AIR EXPOSURE. I CAN MAKE BETTER TIME THROUGH THE HOOP ON MY OWN AND MEET YOU TWO ON MALL LATER.
SEE YOU AROUND.
FINE.
UH...OKAY, RODICE, WE HAVE TO GO UP THE STAIRS NOW— TO GO OUTSIDE...
BEAUTIFUL! BECAUSE, HALO, YOU SEE, THE INSIDE IS THE OUTSIDE. IT'S SO OBVIOUS!
YOU SEE, IT'S LIKE IF YOU IMAGINE THE SOUND OF ONE HAND CLAPPING...
YEAH, WELL, THAT'S REALLY FASCINATING RODICE, BUT COULD YOU JUST CLIMB?
WHAT IS 'UP'? WHAT IS 'DOWN'? ONLY BUDDHA KNOWS THE TRUTH.
HALO, EVERYTHING IS SO CLEAR TO ME NOW.
IT'S LIKE I'VE SEEN THE ULTIMATE VOID!
YEAH?
Tell me about it.

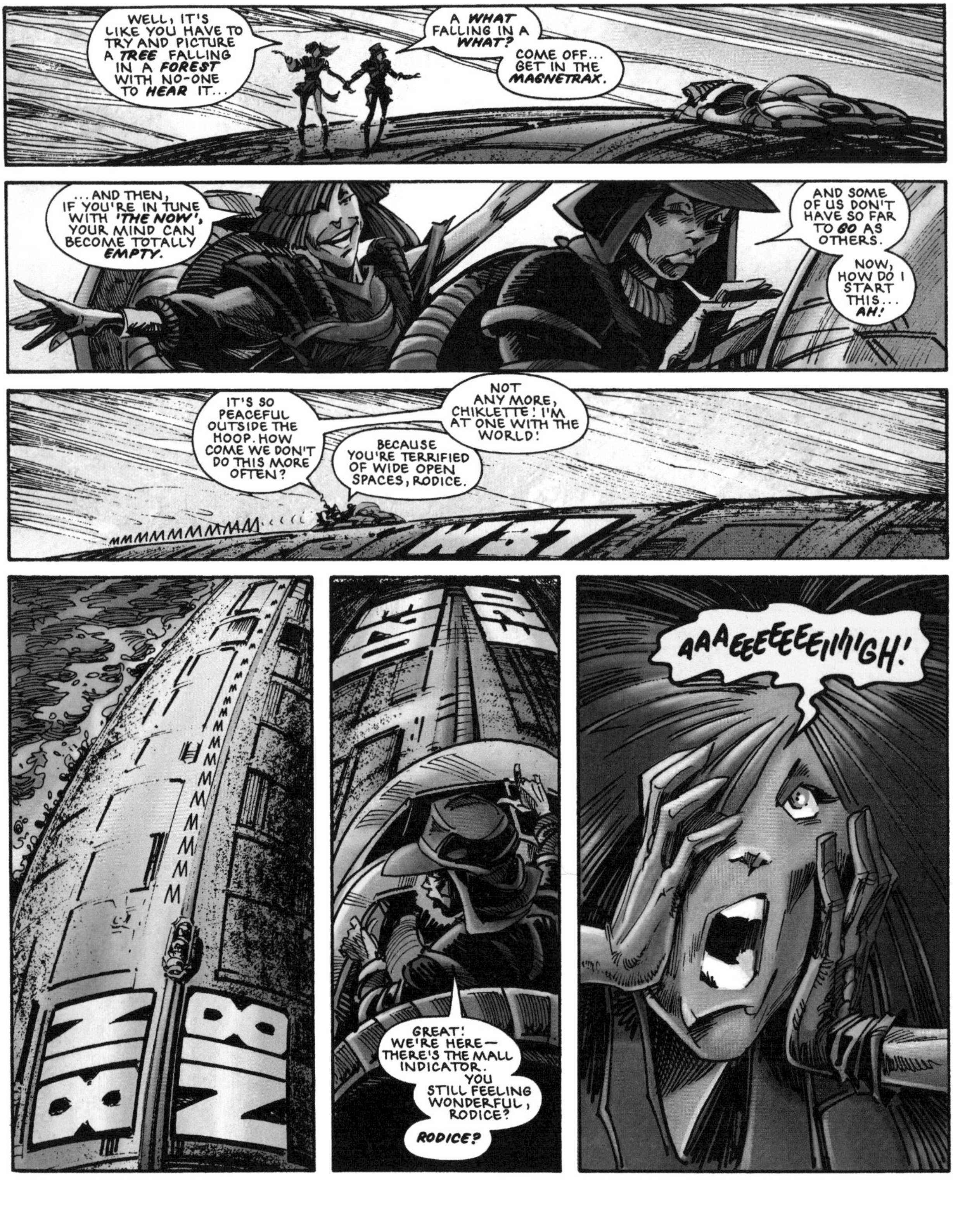

WELL, IT'S LIKE YOU HAVE TO TRY AND PICTURE A TREE FALLING IN A FOREST WITH NO-ONE TO HEAR IT...
A WHAT FALLING IN A WHAT?
COME OFF... GET IN THE MAGNETRAX.
...AND THEN, IF YOU'RE IN TUNE WITH 'THE NOW', YOUR MIND CAN BECOME TOTALLY EMPTY.
AND SOME OF US DON'T HAVE SO FAR TO GO AS OTHERS.
NOW, HOW DO I START THIS... AH!
IT'S SO PEACEFUL OUTSIDE THE HOOP. HOW COME WE DON'T DO THIS MORE OFTEN?
BECAUSE YOU'RE TERRIFIED OF WIDE OPEN SPACES, RODICE.
NOT ANY MORE, CHIKLETTE! I'M AT ONE WITH THE WORLD!
MMMMMMMMMMM
MMMMMMMMMMMMMM
GREAT! WE'RE HERE— THERE'S THE MALL INDICATOR.
YOU STILL FEELING WONDERFUL, RODICE?
RODICE?
AAAEEEEEEIIIIGH!

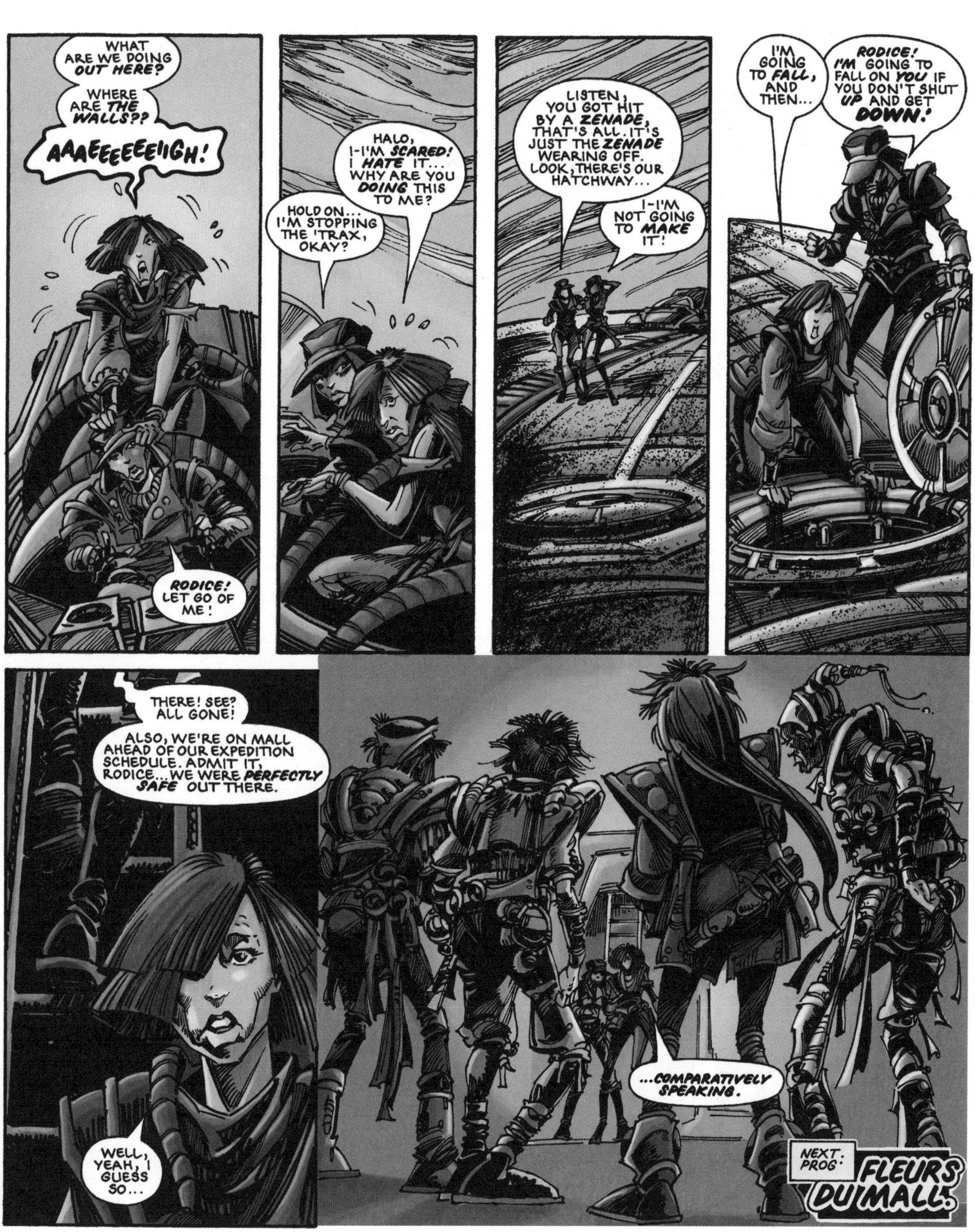
WHAT ARE WE DOING OUT HERE?
WHERE ARE THE WALLS??
AAAEEEEEEEIIGH!
RODICE! LET GO OF ME!
HALO, I-I'M SCARED! I HATE IT... WHY ARE YOU DOING THIS TO ME?
HOLD ON... I'M STOPPING THE 'TRAX, OKAY?
LISTEN, YOU GOT HIT BY A ZENADE, THAT'S ALL. IT'S JUST THE ZENADE WEARING OFF. LOOK, THERE'S OUR HATCHWAY...
I-I'M NOT GOING TO MAKE IT!
I'M GOING TO FALL, AND THEN...
RODICE! I'M GOING TO FALL ON YOU IF YOU DON'T SHUT UP AND GET DOWN!
THERE! SEE? ALL GONE!
ALSO, WE'RE ON MALL AHEAD OF OUR EXPEDITION SCHEDULE. ADMIT IT, RODICE... WE WERE PERFECTLY SAFE OUT THERE.
WELL, YEAH, I GUESS SO...
...COMPARATIVELY SPEAKING.
NEXT PROG: FLEURS DU MALL.

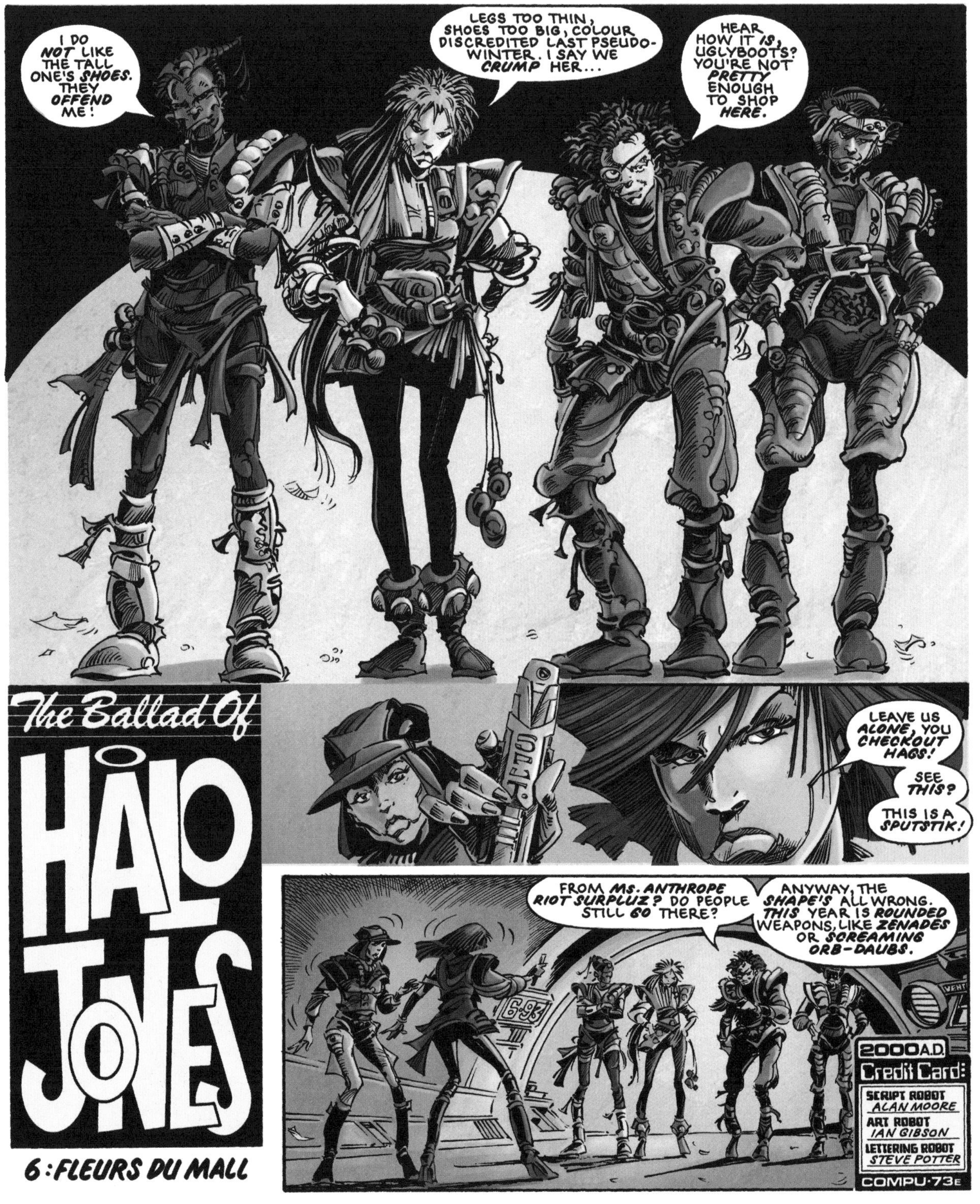
I DO NOT LIKE THE TALL ONE'S SHOES. THEY OFFEND ME!
LEGS TOO THIN, SHOES TOO BIG, COLOUR DISCREDITED LAST PSEUDO-WINTER. I SAY WE CRUMP HER...
HEAR HOW IT IS, UGLYBOOTS? YOU'RE NOT PRETTY ENOUGH TO SHOP HERE.
The Ballad Of
HALO JONES
6: FLEURS DU MALL
LEAVE US ALONE, YOU CHECKOUT HAGS!
SEE THIS?
THIS IS A SPUTSTIK!
FROM MS. ANTHROPE RIOT SURPLUZ? DO PEOPLE STILL GO THERE?
ANYWAY, THE SHAPE'S ALL WRONG. THIS YEAR IS ROUNDED WEAPONS, LIKE ZENADES OR SCREAMING ORB-DAUBS.
2000 A.D.
Credit Card:
SCRIPT ROBOT ALAN MOORE
ART ROBOT IAN GIBSON
LETTERING ROBOT STEVE POTTER
COMPU-73E

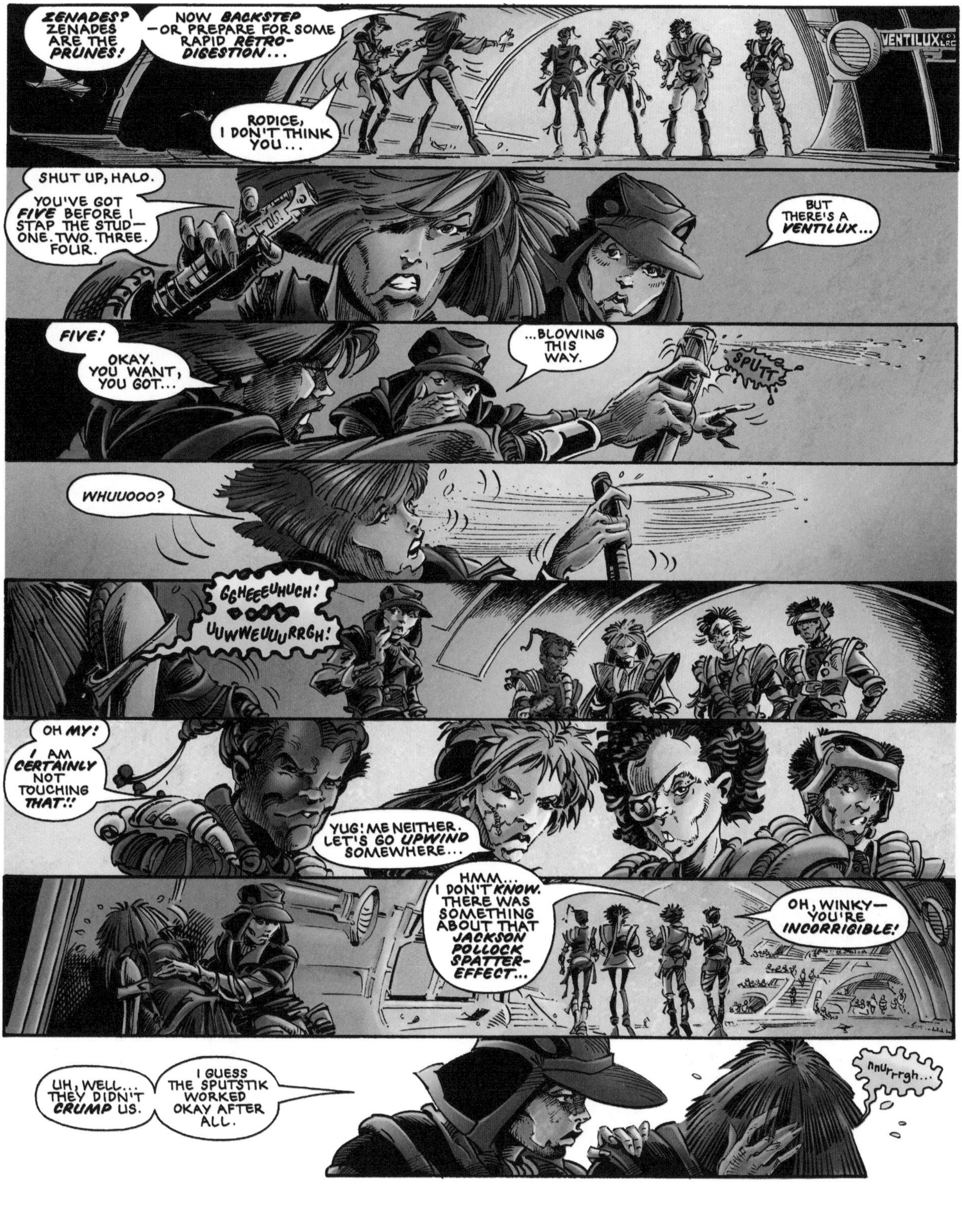
ZENADES? ZENADES ARE THE PRUNES!
NOW BACKSTEP —OR PREPARE FOR SOME RAPID RETRO-DIGESTION...
RODICE, I DON'T THINK YOU...
VENTILUX
SHUT UP, HALO.
YOU'VE GOT FIVE BEFORE I STAP THE STUD— ONE. TWO. THREE. FOUR.
BUT THERE'S A VENTILUX...
FIVE!
OKAY. YOU WANT, YOU GOT...
...BLOWING THIS WAY.
SPUTT
WHUUOOO?
GGHEEEUHUCH! UUWWEUUURRGH!
OH MY! I AM CERTAINLY NOT TOUCHING THAT!!
YUG! ME NEITHER. LET'S GO UPWIND SOMEWHERE...
HMM... I DON'T KNOW. THERE WAS SOMETHING ABOUT THAT JACKSON POLLOCK SPATTER-EFFECT...
OH, WINKY— YOU'RE INCORRIGIBLE!
UH, WELL... THEY DIDN'T CRUMP US.
I GUESS THE SPUTSTIK WORKED OKAY AFTER ALL.
nnUrrrgh...

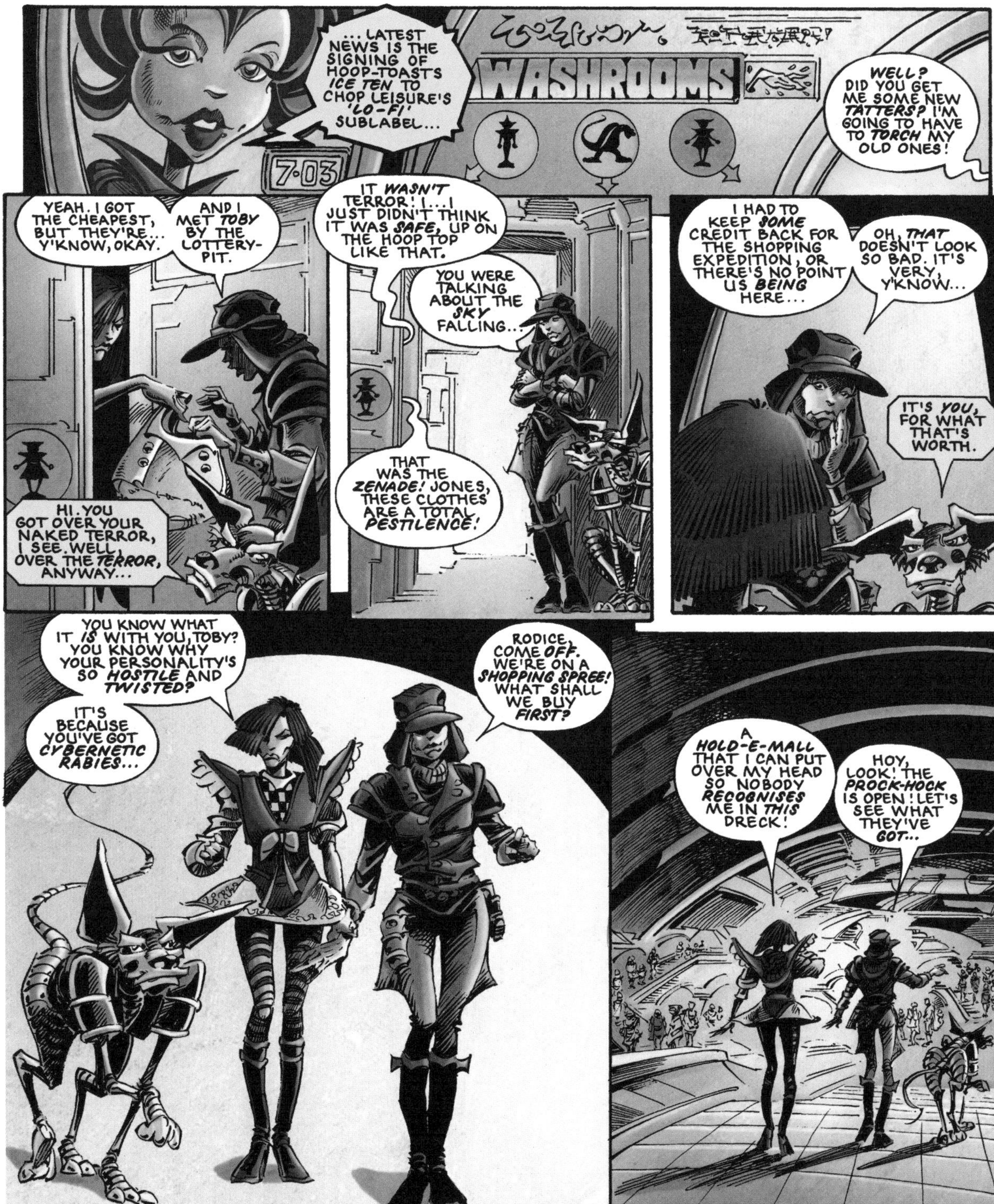
... LATEST NEWS IS THE SIGNING OF HOOP-TOASTS ICE TEN TO CHOP LEISURE'S 'LO-FI' SUBLABEL...
WASHROOMS
7·03
WELL? DID YOU GET ME SOME NEW TATTERS? I'M GOING TO HAVE TO TORCH MY OLD ONES!
YEAH. I GOT THE CHEAPEST, BUT THEY'RE... Y'KNOW, OKAY.
AND I MET TOBY BY THE LOTTERY-PIT.
HI. YOU GOT OVER YOUR NAKED TERROR, I SEE. WELL, OVER THE TERROR, ANYWAY...
IT WASN'T TERROR! I...I JUST DIDN'T THINK IT WAS SAFE, UP ON THE HOOP TOP LIKE THAT.
YOU WERE TALKING ABOUT THE SKY FALLING...
THAT WAS THE ZENADE! JONES, THESE CLOTHES ARE A TOTAL PESTILENCE!
I HAD TO KEEP SOME CREDIT BACK FOR THE SHOPPING EXPEDITION, OR THERE'S NO POINT US BEING HERE...
OH, THAT DOESN'T LOOK SO BAD. IT'S VERY, Y'KNOW...
IT'S YOU, FOR WHAT THAT'S WORTH.
YOU KNOW WHAT IT IS WITH YOU, TOBY? YOU KNOW WHY YOUR PERSONALITY'S SO HOSTILE AND TWISTED?
IT'S BECAUSE YOU'VE GOT CYBERNETIC RABIES...
RODICE, COME OFF. WE'RE ON A SHOPPING SPREE! WHAT SHALL WE BUY FIRST?
A HOLD-E-MALL THAT I CAN PUT OVER MY HEAD SO NOBODY RECOGNISES ME IN THIS DRECK!
HOY, LOOK! THE PROCK-HOCK IS OPEN! LET'S SEE WHAT THEY'VE GOT...

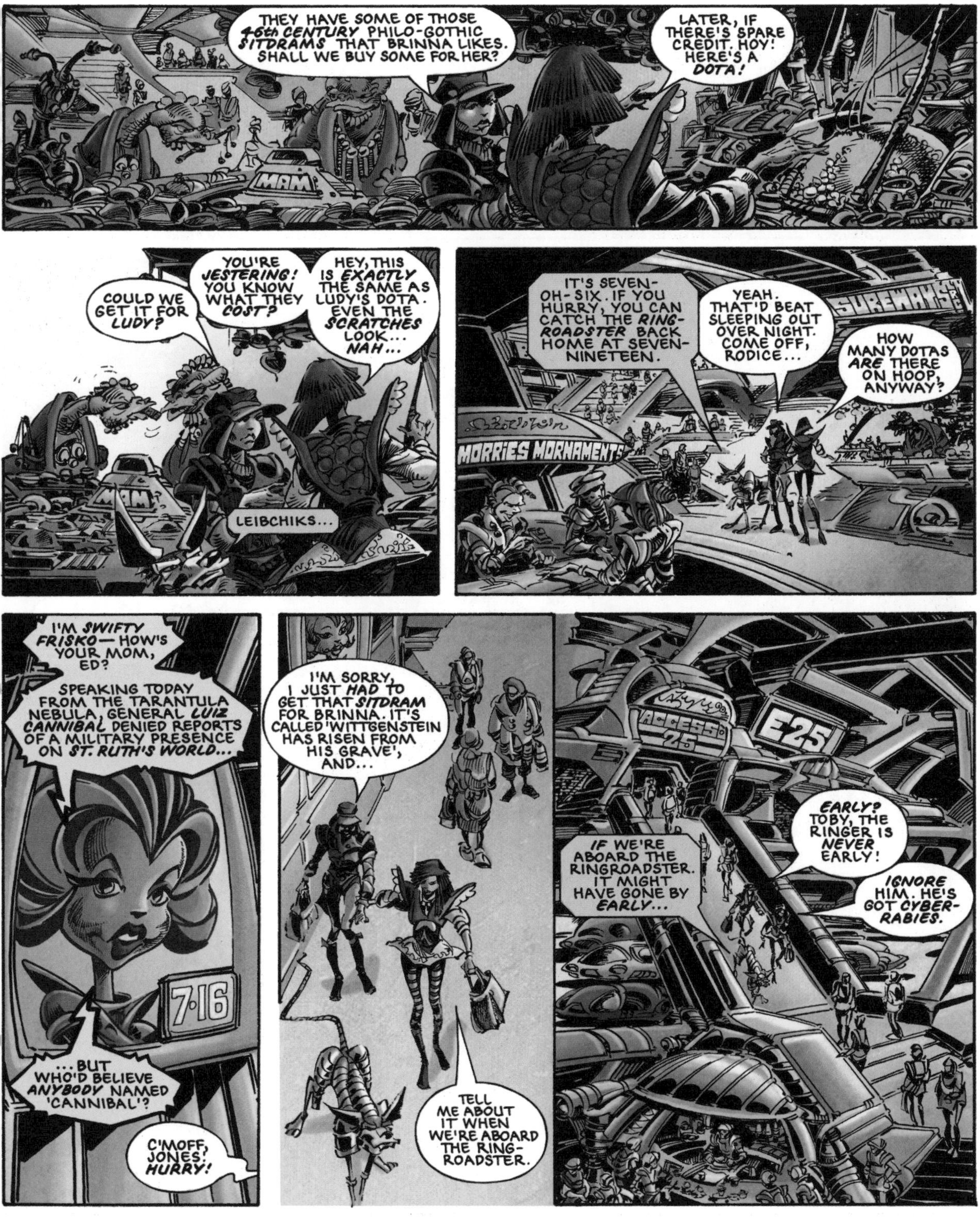
THEY HAVE SOME OF THOSE 46th CENTURY PHILO-GOTHIC SITDRAMS THAT BRINNA LIKES. SHALL WE BUY SOME FOR HER?
LATER, IF THERE'S SPARE CREDIT. HOY! HERE'S A DOTA!
MAM
COULD WE GET IT FOR LUDY?
YOU'RE JESTERING! YOU KNOW WHAT THEY COST?
HEY, THIS IS EXACTLY THE SAME AS LUDY'S DOTA. EVEN THE SCRATCHES LOOK... NAH...
LEIBCHIKS...
MAM
IT'S SEVEN-OH-SIX. IF YOU HURRY, YOU CAN CATCH THE RING-ROADSTER BACK HOME AT SEVEN-NINETEEN.
YEAH. THAT'D BEAT SLEEPING OUT OVER NIGHT. COME OFF, RODICE...
SUREWAYS
HOW MANY DOTAS ARE THERE ON HOOP, ANYWAY?
MORRIES MORNAMENTS
I'M SWIFTY FRISKO— HOW'S YOUR MOM, ED?
SPEAKING TODAY FROM THE TARANTULA NEBULA, GENERAL LUIZ CANNIBAL DENIED REPORTS OF A MILITARY PRESENCE ON ST. RUTH'S WORLD...
7·16
...BUT WHO'D BELIEVE ANYBODY NAMED 'CANNIBAL'?
C'MOFF, JONES! HURRY!
I'M SORRY, I JUST HAD TO GET THAT SITDRAM FOR BRINNA. IT'S CALLED 'WITTGENSTEIN HAS RISEN FROM HIS GRAVE', AND...
TELL ME ABOUT IT WHEN WE'RE ABOARD THE RING-ROADSTER.
ACCESS 25
E-25
IF WE'RE ABOARD THE RINGROADSTER. IT MIGHT HAVE GONE BY EARLY...
EARLY? TOBY, THE RINGER IS NEVER EARLY!
IGNORE HIM. HE'S GOT CYBER-RABIES.

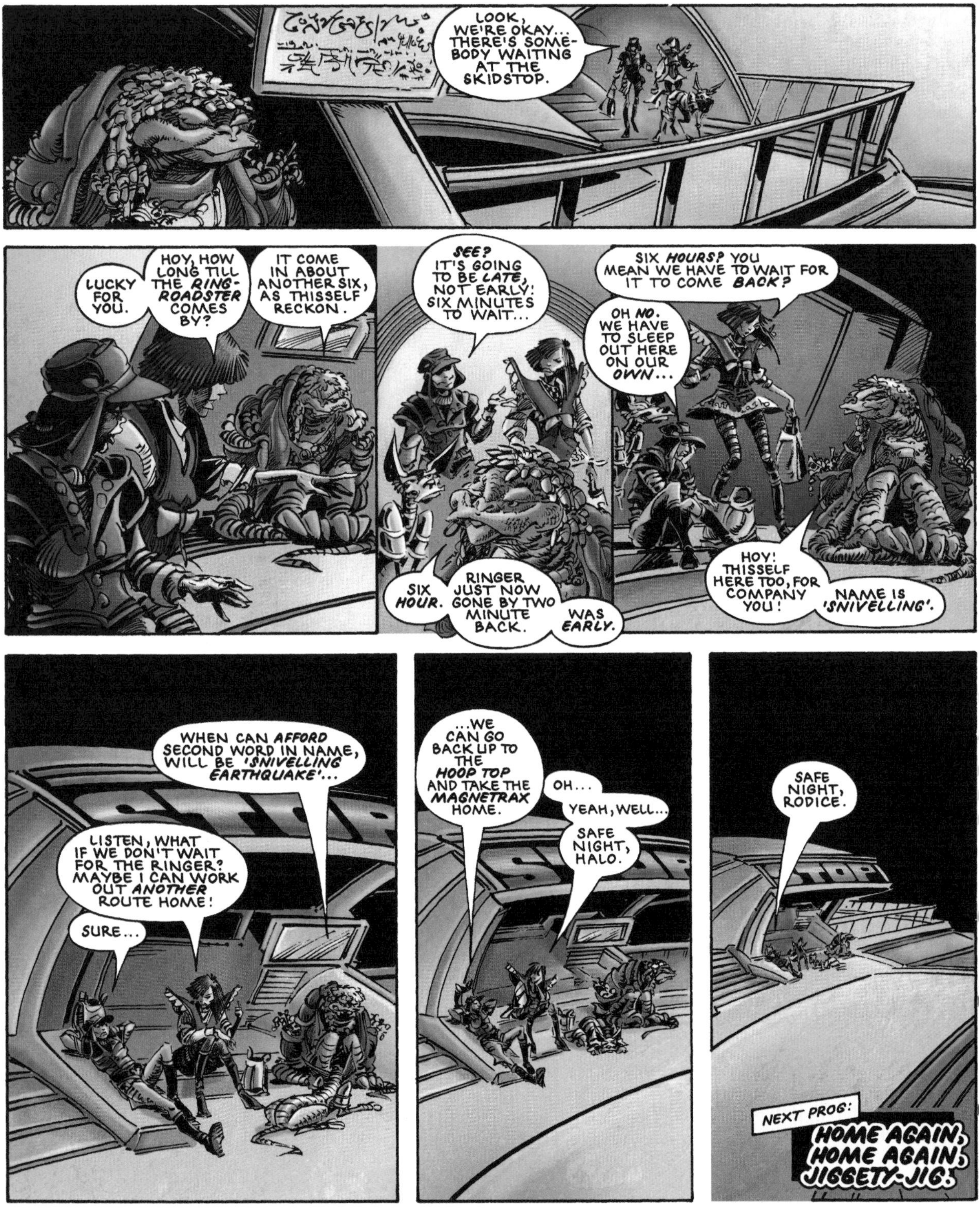
LOOK, WE'RE OKAY... THERE'S SOMEBODY WAITING AT THE SKIDSTOP.
LUCKY FOR YOU.
HOY, HOW LONG TILL THE RING-ROADSTER COMES BY?
IT COME IN ABOUT ANOTHER SIX, AS THISSELF RECKON.
SEE? IT'S GOING TO BE LATE, NOT EARLY! SIX MINUTES TO WAIT...
SIX HOUR.
RINGER JUST NOW GONE BY TWO MINUTE BACK.
WAS EARLY.
SIX HOURS? YOU MEAN WE HAVE TO WAIT FOR IT TO COME BACK?
OH NO. WE HAVE TO SLEEP OUT HERE ON OUR OWN...
HOY! THISSELF HERE TOO, FOR COMPANY YOU!
NAME IS 'SNIVELLING'.
WHEN CAN AFFORD SECOND WORD IN NAME, WILL BE 'SNIVELLING EARTHQUAKE'...
LISTEN, WHAT IF WE DON'T WAIT FOR THE RINGER? MAYBE I CAN WORK OUT ANOTHER ROUTE HOME!
SURE...
...WE CAN GO BACK UP TO THE HOOP TOP AND TAKE THE MAGNETRAX HOME.
OH...
YEAH, WELL...
SAFE NIGHT, HALO.
SAFE NIGHT, RODICE.
NEXT PROG:
HOME AGAIN, HOME AGAIN, JIGGETY-JIG.

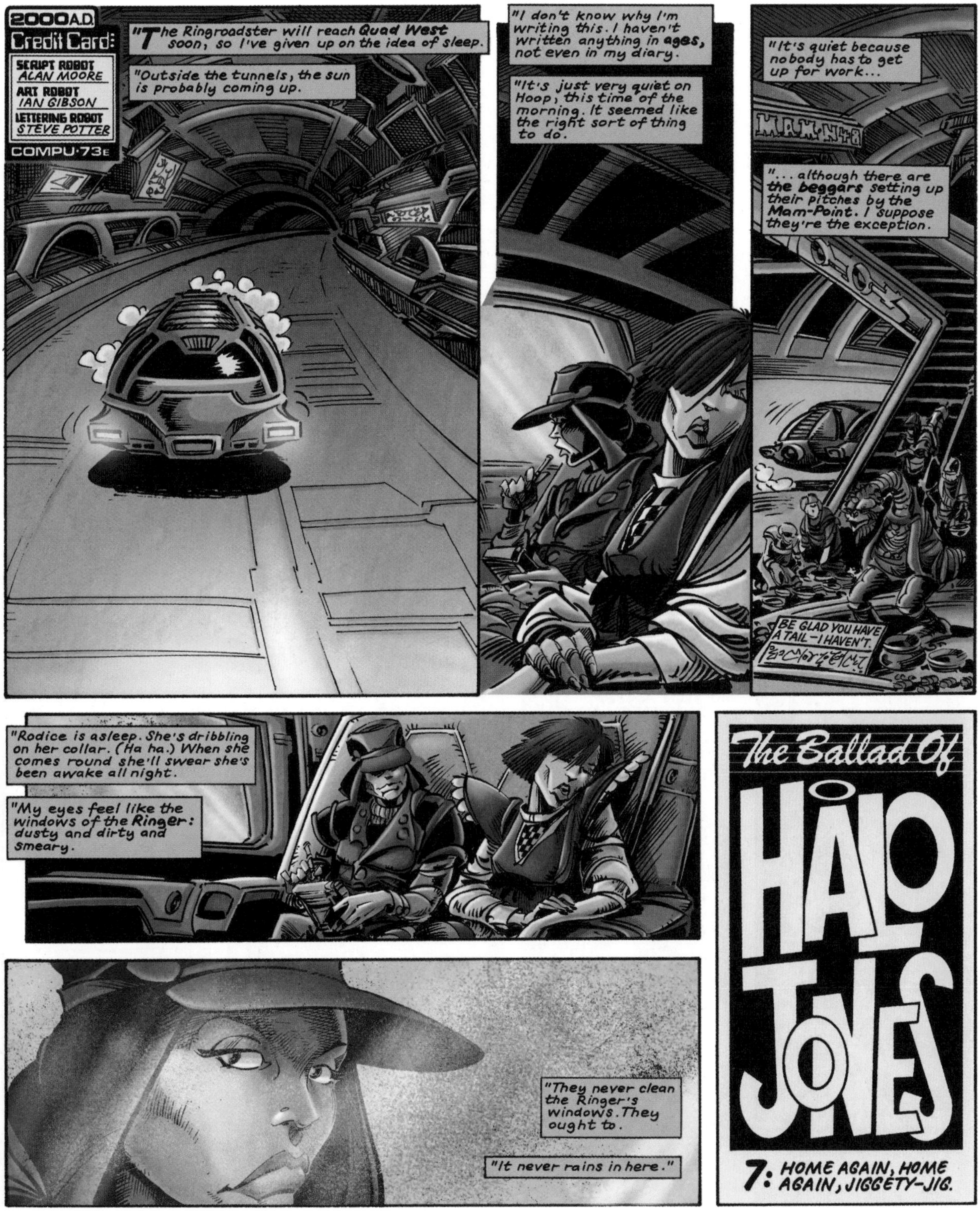
2000 A.D.
Credit Card:
SCRIPT ROBOT ALAN MOORE
ART ROBOT IAN GIBSON
LETTERING ROBOT STEVE POTTER
COMPU·73E
"The Ringroadster will reach Quad West soon, so I've given up on the idea of sleep.
"Outside the tunnels, the sun is probably coming up.
"I don't know why I'm writing this. I haven't written anything in ages, not even in my diary.
"It's just very quiet on Hoop, this time of the morning. It seemed like the right sort of thing to do.
"It's quiet because nobody has to get up for work...
"... although there are the beggars setting up their pitches by the Mam-Point. I suppose they're the exception.
BE GLAD YOU HAVE A TAIL–I HAVEN'T.
"Rodice is asleep. She's dribbling on her collar. (Ha ha.) When she comes round she'll swear she's been awake all night.
"My eyes feel like the windows of the Ringer: dusty and dirty and smeary.
The Ballad Of
HALO JONES
7: HOME AGAIN, HOME AGAIN, JIGGETY-JIG.
"They never clean the Ringer's windows. They ought to.
"It never rains in here."

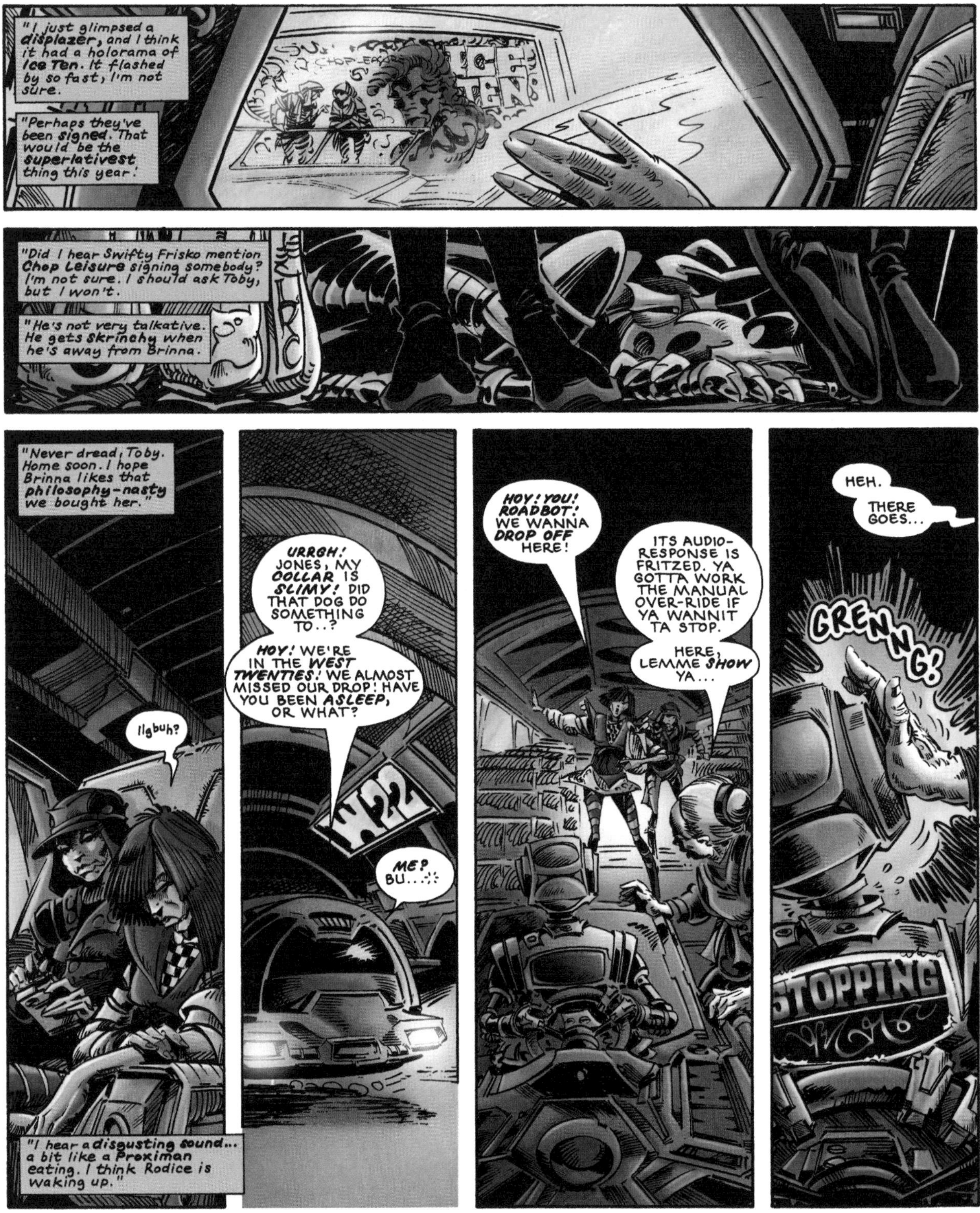

"I just glimpsed a displazer, and I think it had a holorama of Ice Ten. It flashed by so fast, I'm not sure.
"Perhaps they've been signed. That would be the superlativest thing this year!
"Did I hear Swifty Frisko mention Chop Leisure signing somebody? I'm not sure. I should ask Toby, but I won't.
"He's not very talkative. He gets skrinchy when he's away from Brinna.
"Never dread, Toby. Home soon. I hope Brinna likes that philosophy-nasty we bought her."
Ilgbuh?
"I hear a disgusting sound... a bit like a Proximan eating. I think Rodice is waking up."
URRGH! JONES, MY COLLAR IS SLIMY! DID THAT DOG DO SOMETHING TO..?
HOY! WE'RE IN THE WEST TWENTIES! WE ALMOST MISSED OUR DROP! HAVE YOU BEEN ASLEEP, OR WHAT?
W.22
ME? BU...
HOY! YOU! ROADBOT! WE WANNA DROP OFF HERE!
ITS AUDIO-RESPONSE IS FRITZED. YA GOTTA WORK THE MANUAL OVER-RIDE IF YA WANNIT TA STOP.
HERE, LEMME SHOW YA...
HEH.
THERE GOES...
GRENNNG!
STOPPING

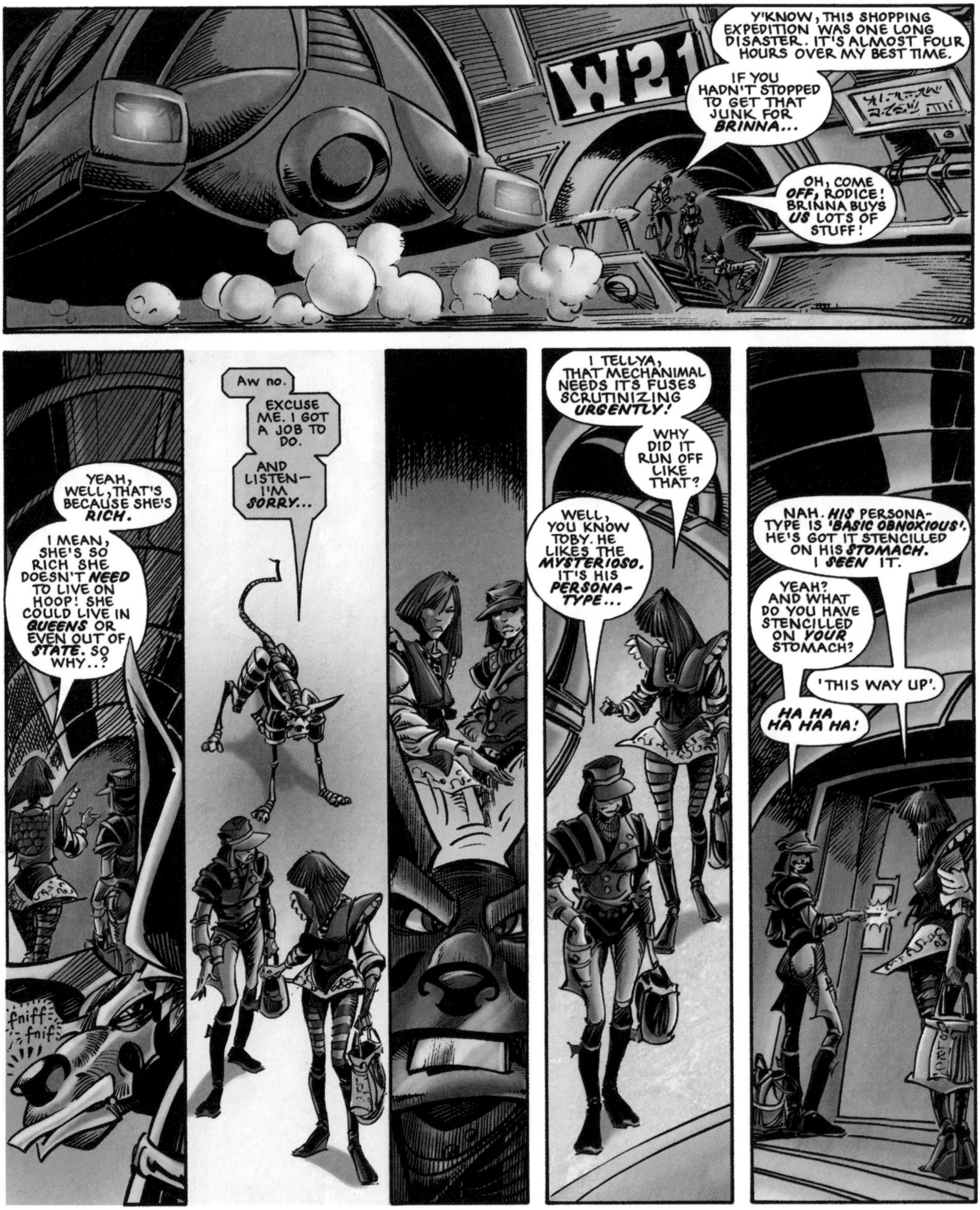
Y'KNOW, THIS SHOPPING EXPEDITION WAS ONE LONG DISASTER. IT'S ALMOST FOUR HOURS OVER MY BEST TIME.
IF YOU HADN'T STOPPED TO GET THAT JUNK FOR BRINNA...
OH, COME OFF, RODICE! BRINNA BUYS US LOTS OF STUFF!
W21
YEAH, WELL, THAT'S BECAUSE SHE'S RICH.
I MEAN, SHE'S SO RICH SHE DOESN'T NEED TO LIVE ON HOOP! SHE COULD LIVE IN QUEENS OR EVEN OUT OF STATE. SO WHY..?
fniff fnif
Aw no.
EXCUSE ME. I GOT A JOB TO DO.
AND LISTEN— I'M SORRY...
I TELLYA, THAT MECHANIMAL NEEDS ITS FUSES SCRUTINIZING URGENTLY!
WHY DID IT RUN OFF LIKE THAT?
WELL, YOU KNOW TOBY. HE LIKES THE MYSTERIOSO. IT'S HIS PERSONA-TYPE...
NAH. HIS PERSONA-TYPE IS 'BASIC OBNOXIOUS'. HE'S GOT IT STENCILLED ON HIS STOMACH. I SEEN IT.
YEAH? AND WHAT DO YOU HAVE STENCILLED ON YOUR STOMACH?
'THIS WAY UP'.
HA HA HA HA HA!

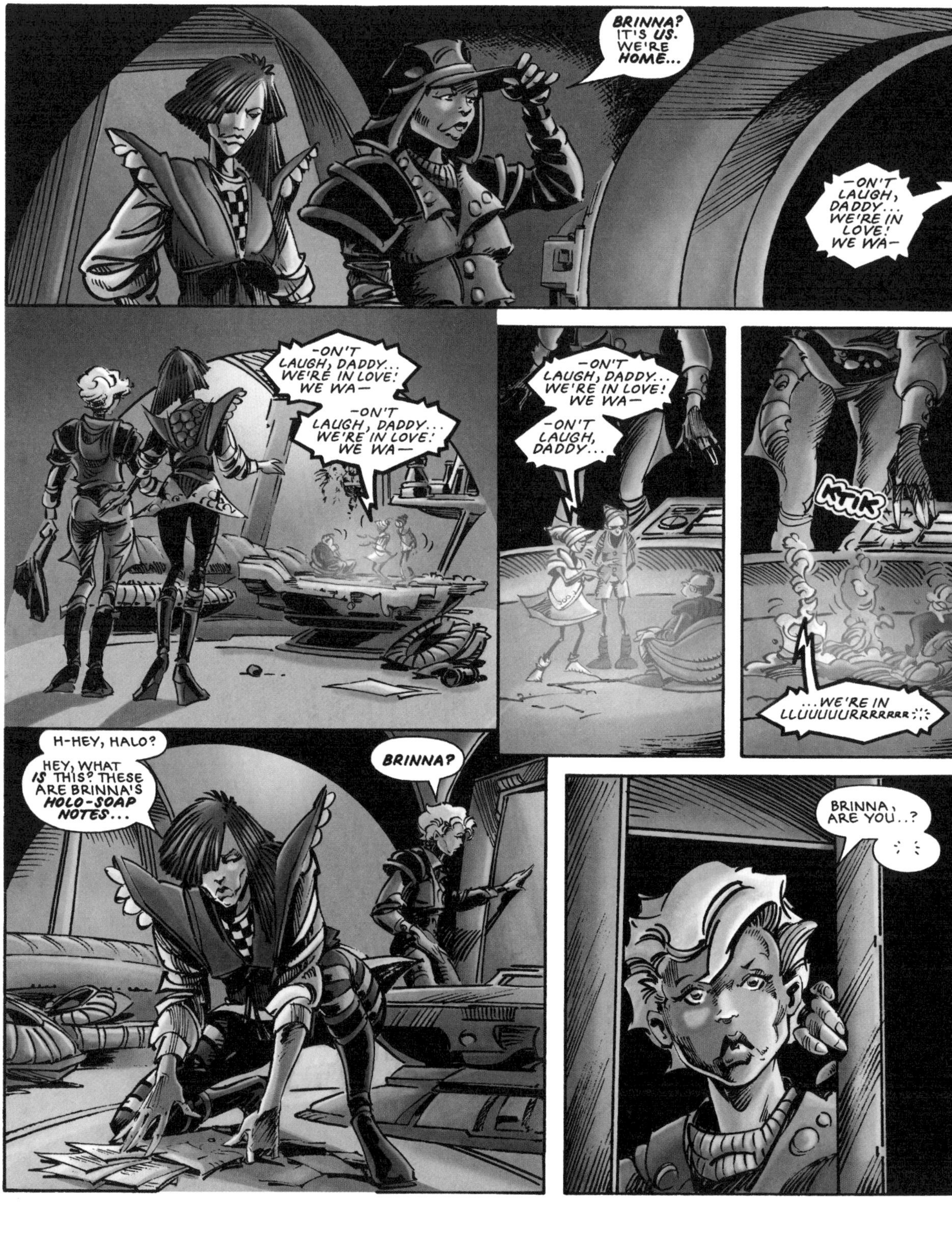
BRINNA? IT'S US. WE'RE HOME...
—ON'T LAUGH, DADDY... WE'RE IN LOVE! WE WA—
—ON'T LAUGH, DADDY... WE'RE IN LOVE! WE WA—
—ON'T LAUGH, DADDY... WE'RE IN LOVE! WE WA—
—ON'T LAUGH, DADDY... WE'RE IN LOVE! WE WA—
—ON'T LAUGH, DADDY...
KTIK
...WE'RE IN LLUUUUURRRRRRR
H-HEY, HALO?
HEY, WHAT IS THIS? THESE ARE BRINNA'S HOLO-SOAP NOTES...
BRINNA?
BRINNA, ARE YOU..?

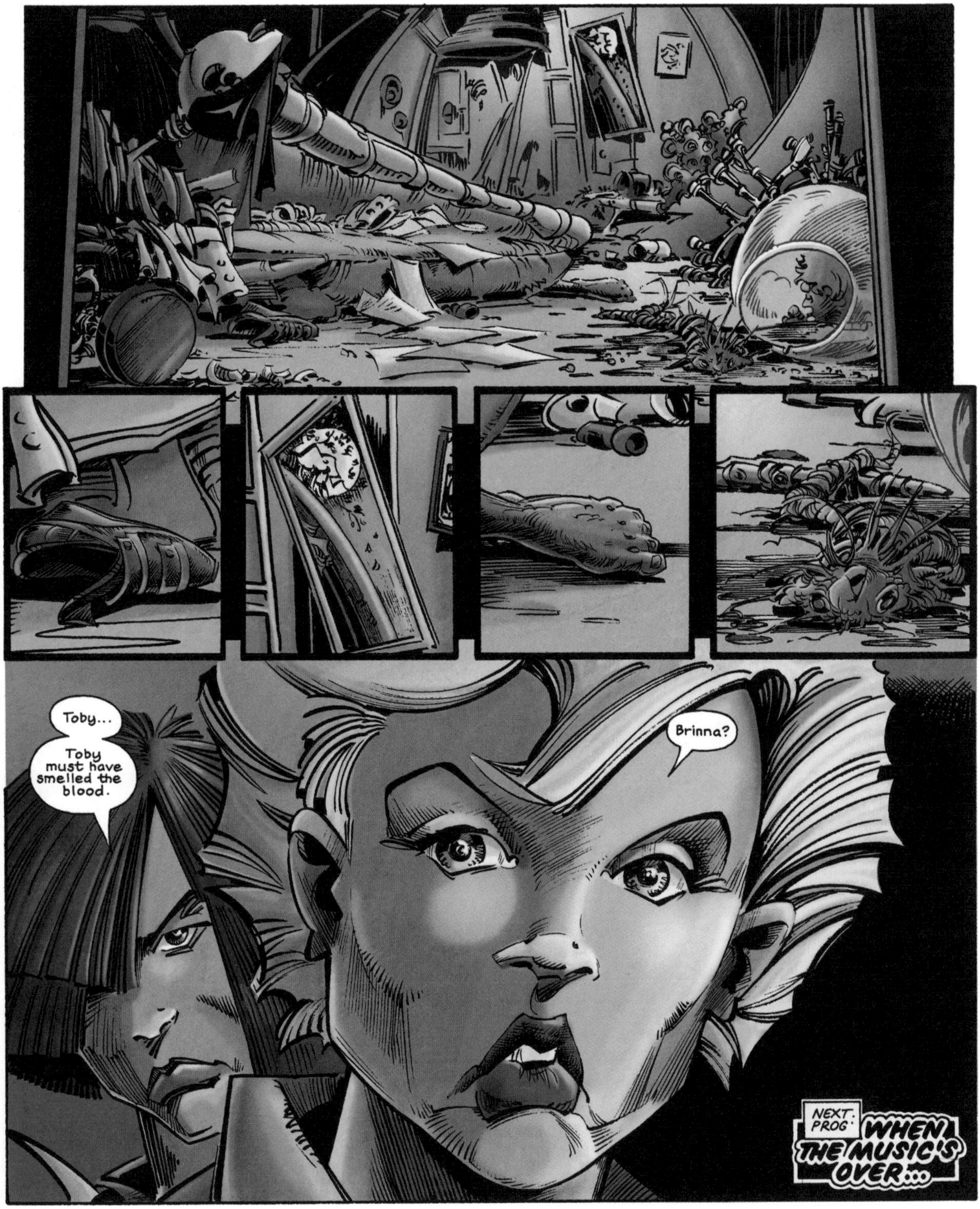
Toby...
Toby must have smelled the blood.
Brinna?
NEXT PROG: WHEN THE MUSIC'S OVER...

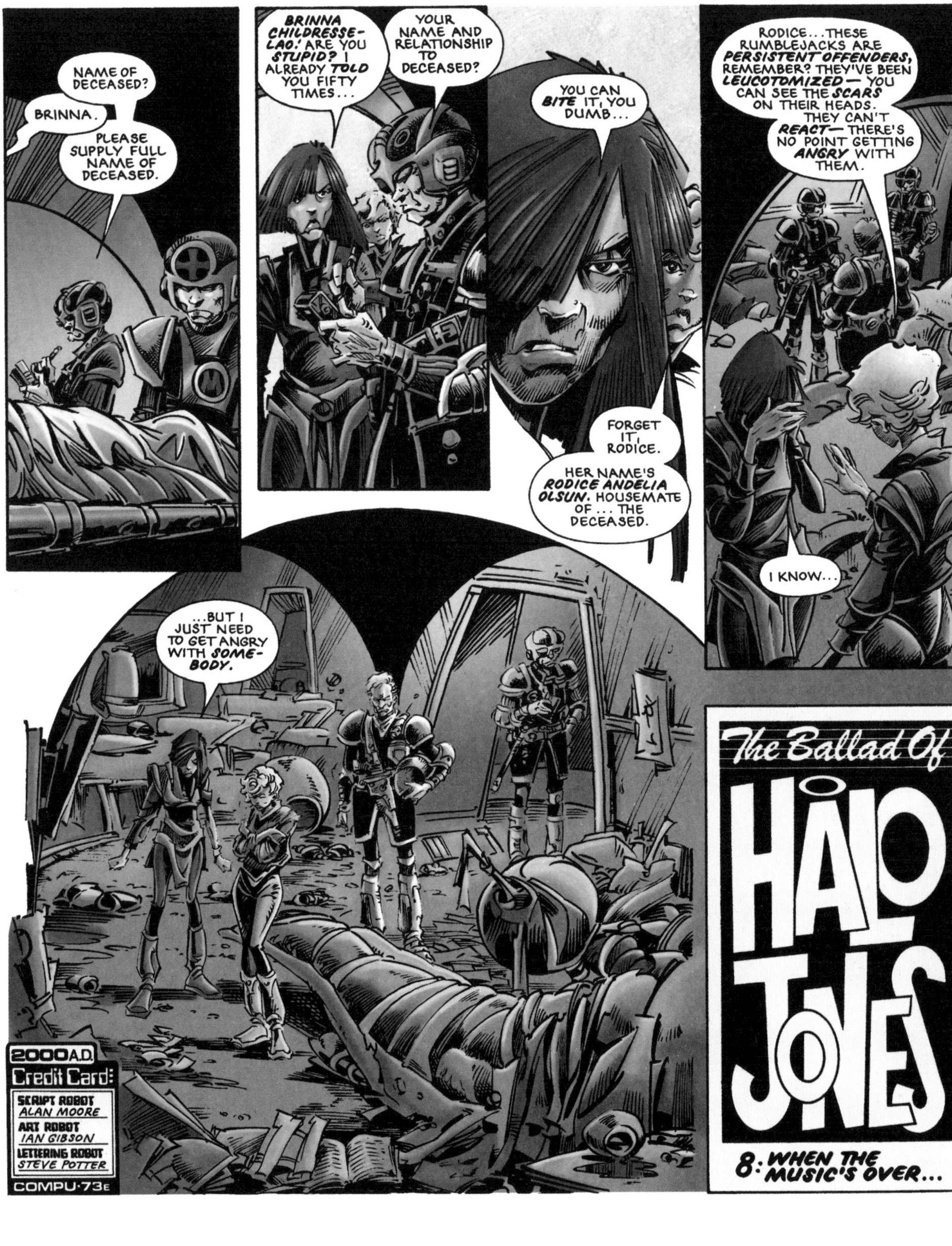
NAME OF DECEASED?
BRINNA.
PLEASE SUPPLY FULL NAME OF DECEASED.
BRINNA CHILDRESSE-LAO! ARE YOU STUPID? I ALREADY TOLD YOU FIFTY TIMES...
YOUR NAME AND RELATIONSHIP TO DECEASED?
YOU CAN BITE IT, YOU DUMB...
FORGET IT, RODICE.
HER NAME'S RODICE ANDELIA OLSUN. HOUSEMATE OF ... THE DECEASED.
RODICE... THESE RUMBLEJACKS ARE PERSISTENT OFFENDERS, REMEMBER? THEY'VE BEEN LEUCOTOMIZED — YOU CAN SEE THE SCARS ON THEIR HEADS.
THEY CAN'T REACT — THERE'S NO POINT GETTING ANGRY WITH THEM.
I KNOW...
...BUT I JUST NEED TO GET ANGRY WITH SOMEBODY.
2000 A.D.
Credit Card:
SCRIPT ROBOT ALAN MOORE
ART ROBOT IAN GIBSON
LETTERING ROBOT STEVE POTTER
COMPU-73E
The Ballad Of
HALO JONES
8: WHEN THE MUSIC'S OVER...

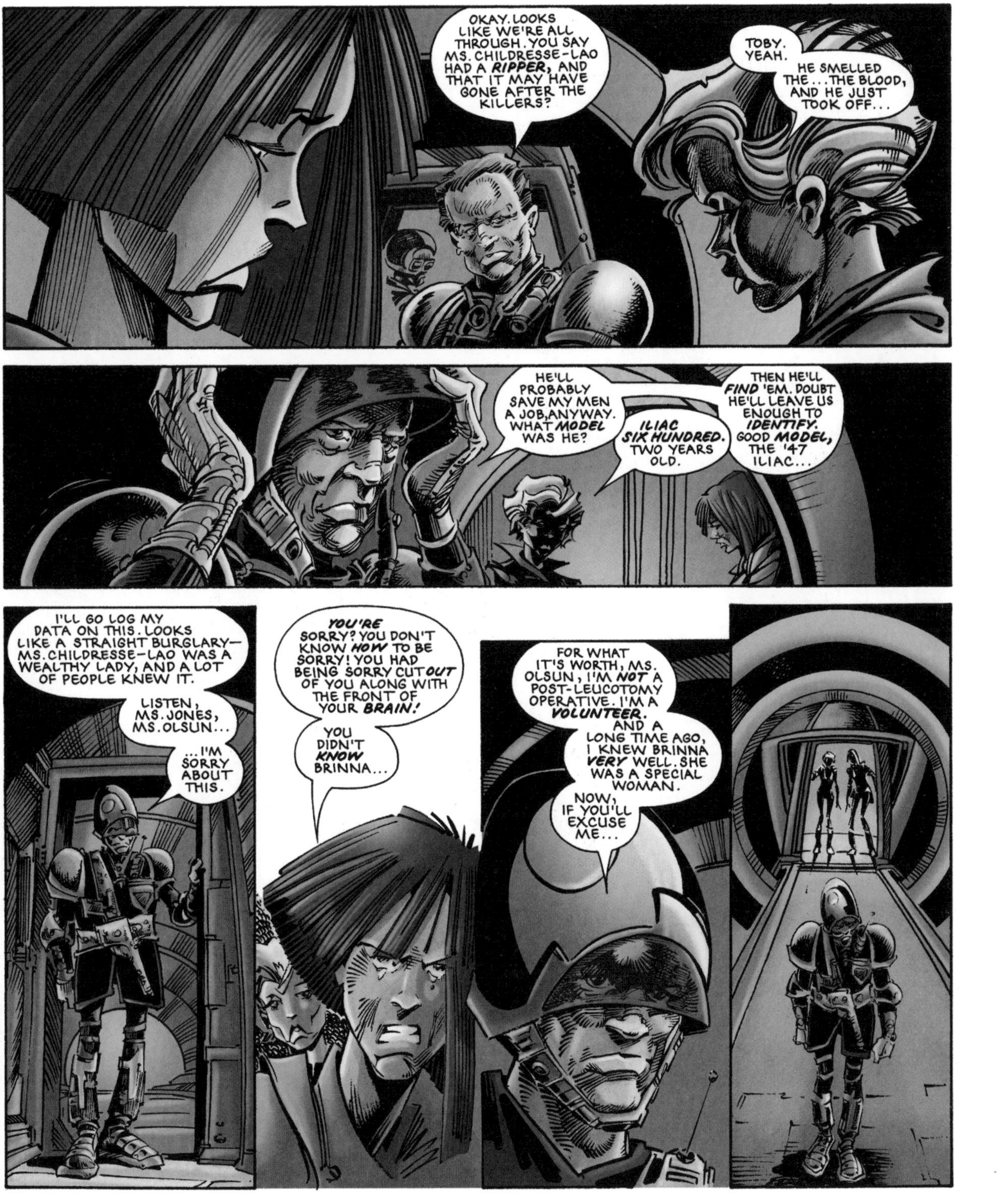

OKAY. LOOKS LIKE WE'RE ALL THROUGH. YOU SAY MS. CHILDRESSE-LAO HAD A RIPPER, AND THAT IT MAY HAVE GONE AFTER THE KILLERS?
TOBY. YEAH.
HE SMELLED THE... THE BLOOD, AND HE JUST TOOK OFF...
HE'LL PROBABLY SAVE MY MEN A JOB, ANYWAY. WHAT MODEL WAS HE?
ILIAC SIX HUNDRED. TWO YEARS OLD.
THEN HE'LL FIND 'EM. DOUBT HE'LL LEAVE US ENOUGH TO IDENTIFY. GOOD MODEL, THE '47 ILIAC...
I'LL GO LOG MY DATA ON THIS. LOOKS LIKE A STRAIGHT BURGLARY--MS. CHILDRESSE-LAO WAS A WEALTHY LADY, AND A LOT OF PEOPLE KNEW IT.
LISTEN, MS. JONES, MS. OLSUN...
...I'M SORRY ABOUT THIS.
YOU'RE SORRY? YOU DON'T KNOW HOW TO BE SORRY! YOU HAD BEING SORRY CUT OUT OF YOU ALONG WITH THE FRONT OF YOUR BRAIN!
YOU DIDN'T KNOW BRINNA...
FOR WHAT IT'S WORTH, MS. OLSUN, I'M NOT A POST-LEUCOTOMY OPERATIVE. I'M A VOLUNTEER.
AND A LONG TIME AGO, I KNEW BRINNA VERY WELL. SHE WAS A SPECIAL WOMAN.
NOW, IF YOU'LL EXCUSE ME...

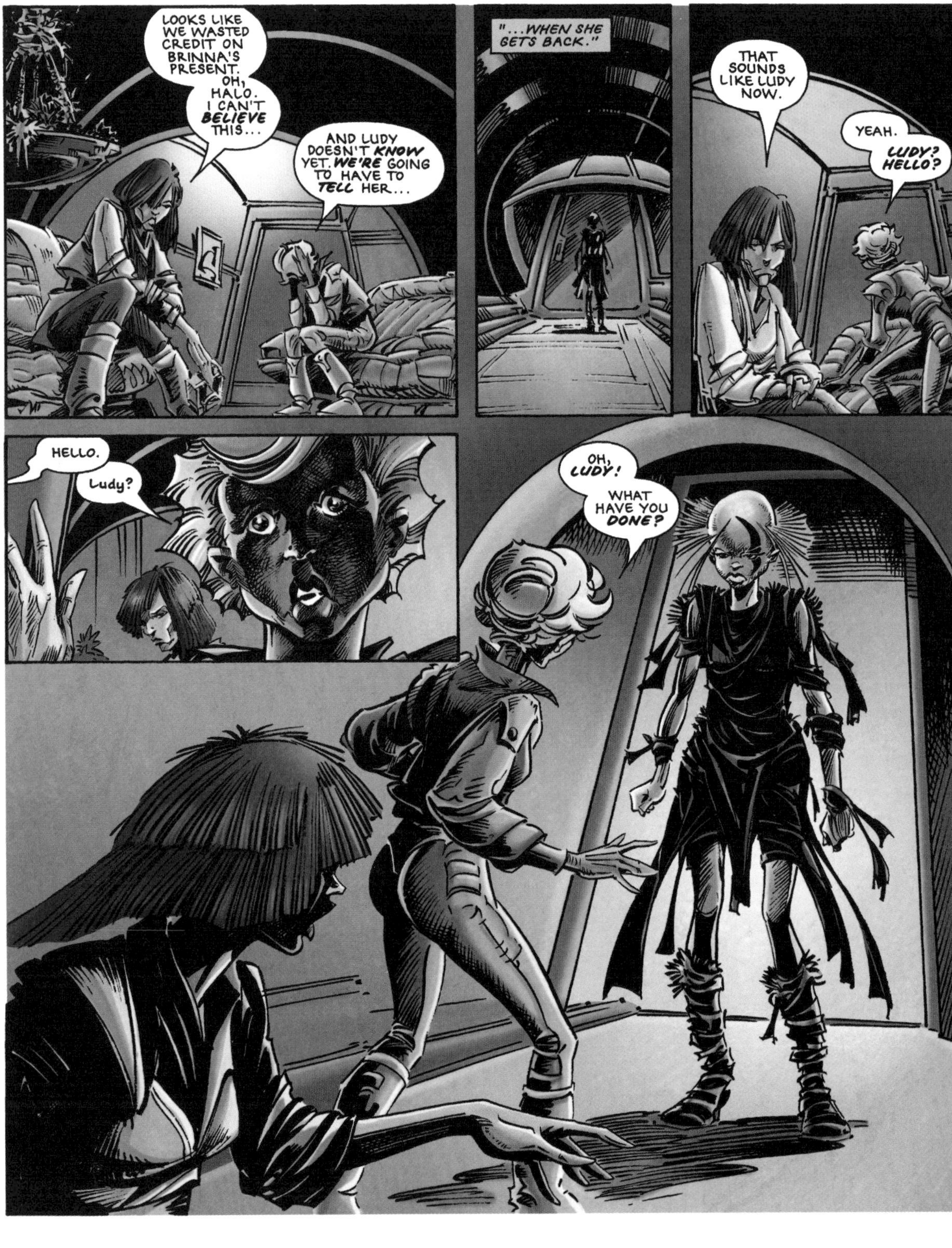
LOOKS LIKE WE WASTED CREDIT ON BRINNA'S PRESENT.
OH, HALO. I CAN'T BELIEVE THIS...
AND LUDY DOESN'T KNOW YET. WE'RE GOING TO HAVE TO TELL HER...
"...WHEN SHE GETS BACK."
THAT SOUNDS LIKE LUDY NOW.
YEAH.
LUDY? HELLO?
HELLO.
Ludy?
OH, LUDY!
WHAT HAVE YOU DONE?

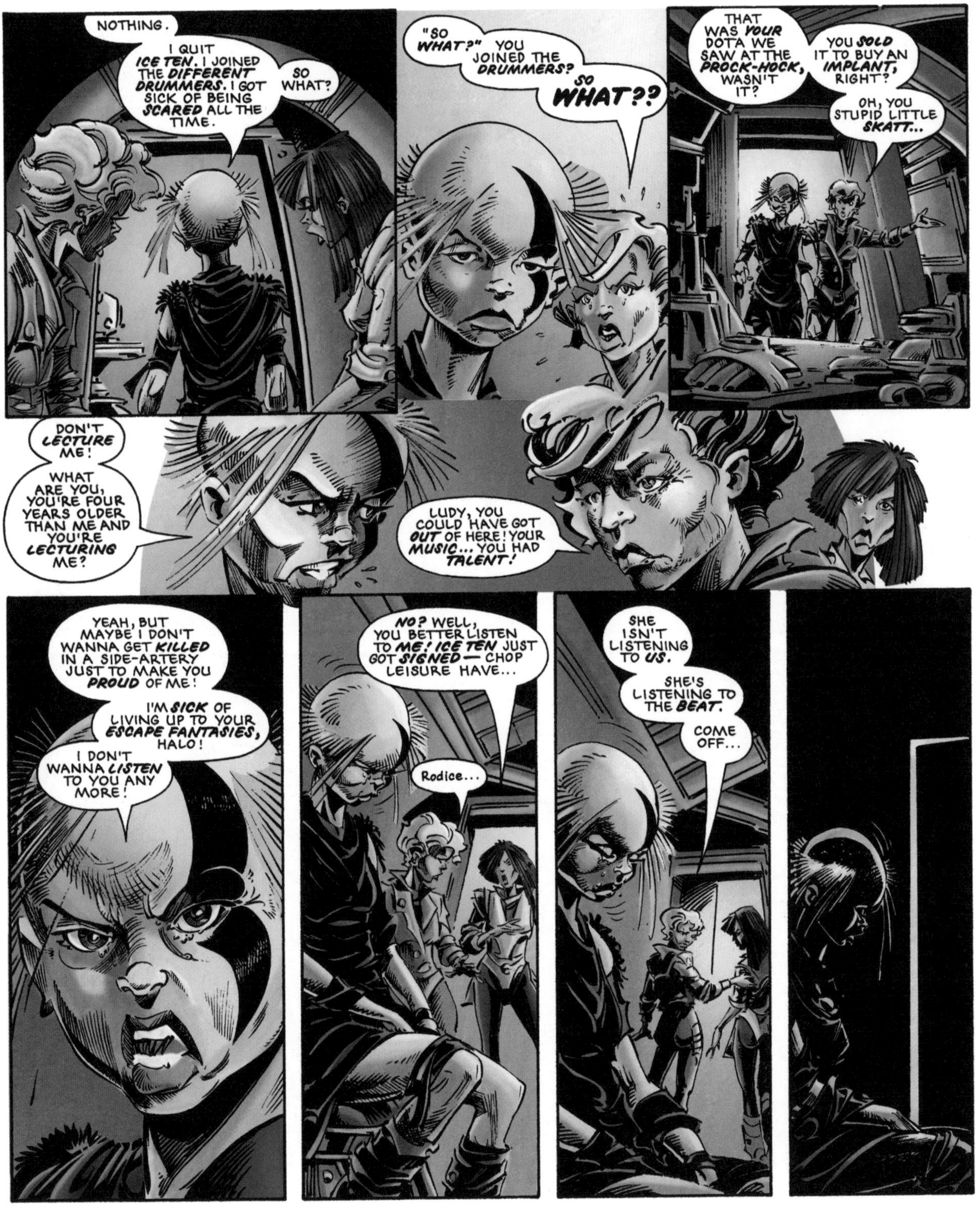
NOTHING.
I QUIT ICE TEN. I JOINED THE DIFFERENT DRUMMERS. I GOT SICK OF BEING SCARED ALL THE TIME.
SO WHAT?
"SO WHAT?" YOU JOINED THE DRUMMERS?
SO WHAT??
THAT WAS YOUR DOTA WE SAW AT THE PROCK-HOCK, WASN'T IT?
YOU SOLD IT TO BUY AN IMPLANT, RIGHT?
OH, YOU STUPID LITTLE SKATT...
DON'T LECTURE ME!
WHAT ARE YOU, YOU'RE FOUR YEARS OLDER THAN ME AND YOU'RE LECTURING ME?
LUDY, YOU COULD HAVE GOT OUT OF HERE! YOUR MUSIC... YOU HAD TALENT!
YEAH, BUT MAYBE I DON'T WANNA GET KILLED IN A SIDE-ARTERY JUST TO MAKE YOU PROUD OF ME!
I'M SICK OF LIVING UP TO YOUR ESCAPE FANTASIES, HALO!
I DON'T WANNA LISTEN TO YOU ANY MORE!
NO? WELL, YOU BETTER LISTEN TO ME! ICE TEN JUST GOT SIGNED — CHOP LEISURE HAVE...
Rodice...
SHE ISN'T LISTENING TO US.
SHE'S LISTENING TO THE BEAT.
COME OFF...

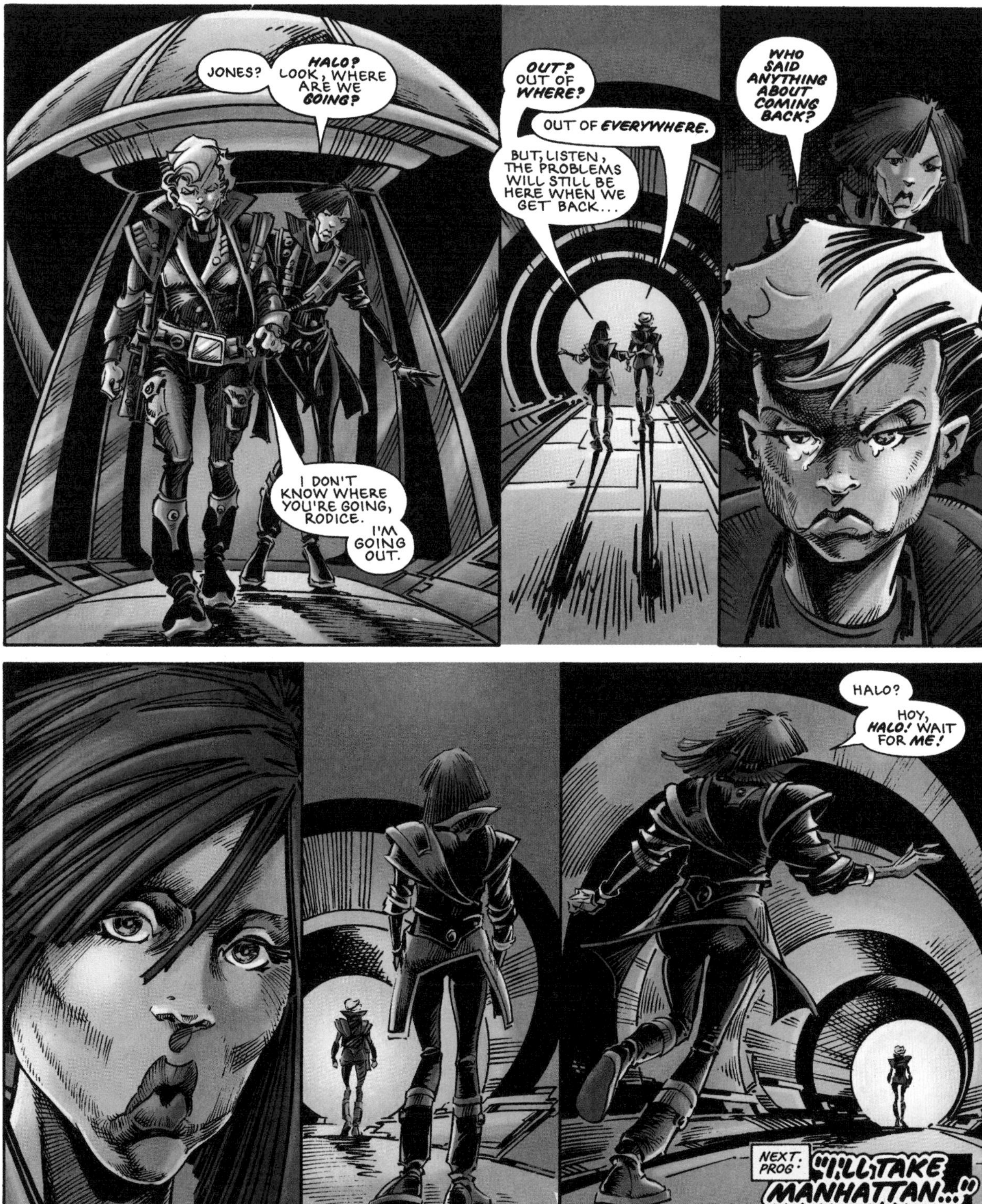
JONES?
HALO? LOOK, WHERE ARE WE GOING?
I DON'T KNOW WHERE YOU'RE GOING, RODICE.
I'M GOING OUT.
OUT? OUT OF WHERE?
OUT OF EVERYWHERE.
BUT, LISTEN, THE PROBLEMS WILL STILL BE HERE WHEN WE GET BACK...
WHO SAID ANYTHING ABOUT COMING BACK?
HALO?
HOY, HALO! WAIT FOR ME!
NEXT PROG: "I'LL TAKE MANHATTAN..."

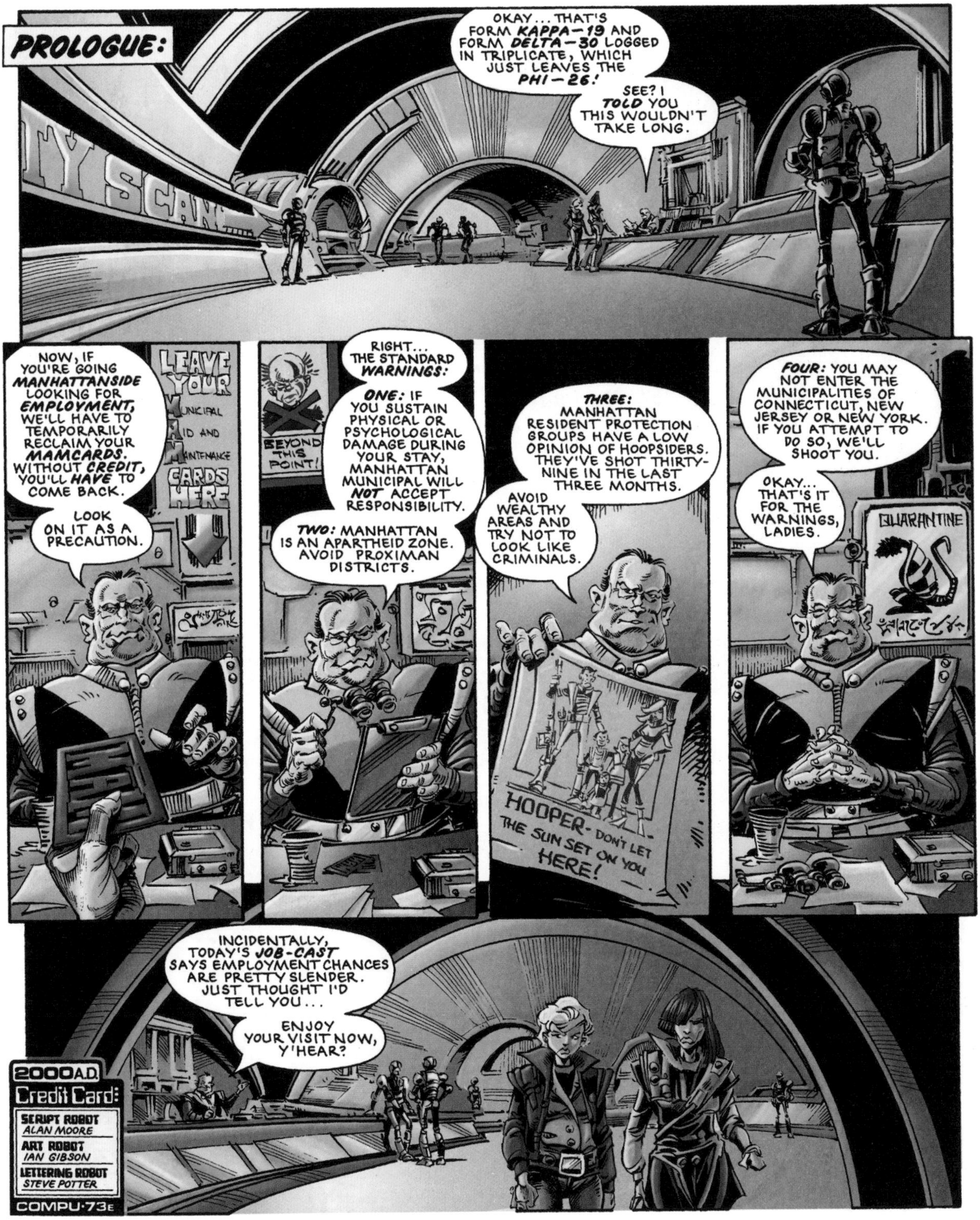
PROLOGUE:
OKAY... THAT'S FORM KAPPA-19 AND FORM DELTA-30 LOGGED IN TRIPLICATE, WHICH JUST LEAVES THE PHI-26!
SEE? I TOLD YOU THIS WOULDN'T TAKE LONG.
LEAVE YOUR M UNICIPAL A ID AND M AINTENANCE CARDS HERE
NOW, IF YOU'RE GOING MANHATTANSIDE LOOKING FOR EMPLOYMENT, WE'LL HAVE TO TEMPORARILY RECLAIM YOUR MAMCARDS. WITHOUT CREDIT, YOU'LL HAVE TO COME BACK.
LOOK ON IT AS A PRECAUTION.
BEYOND THIS POINT!
RIGHT... THE STANDARD WARNINGS:
ONE: IF YOU SUSTAIN PHYSICAL OR PSYCHOLOGICAL DAMAGE DURING YOUR STAY, MANHATTAN MUNICIPAL WILL NOT ACCEPT RESPONSIBILITY.
TWO: MANHATTAN IS AN APARTHEID ZONE. AVOID PROXIMAN DISTRICTS.
THREE: MANHATTAN RESIDENT PROTECTION GROUPS HAVE A LOW OPINION OF HOOPSIDERS. THEY'VE SHOT THIRTY-NINE IN THE LAST THREE MONTHS.
AVOID WEALTHY AREAS AND TRY NOT TO LOOK LIKE CRIMINALS.
HOOPER- DON'T LET THE SUN SET ON YOU HERE!
FOUR: YOU MAY NOT ENTER THE MUNICIPALITIES OF CONNECTICUT, NEW JERSEY OR NEW YORK. IF YOU ATTEMPT TO DO SO, WE'LL SHOOT YOU.
OKAY... THAT'S IT FOR THE WARNINGS, LADIES.
QUARANTINE
INCIDENTALLY, TODAY'S JOB-CAST SAYS EMPLOYMENT CHANCES ARE PRETTY SLENDER. JUST THOUGHT I'D TELL YOU...
ENJOY YOUR VISIT NOW, Y'HEAR?
2000 A.D. Credit Card:
SCRIPT ROBOT ALAN MOORE
ART ROBOT IAN GIBSON
LETTERING ROBOT STEVE POTTER
COMPU-73E

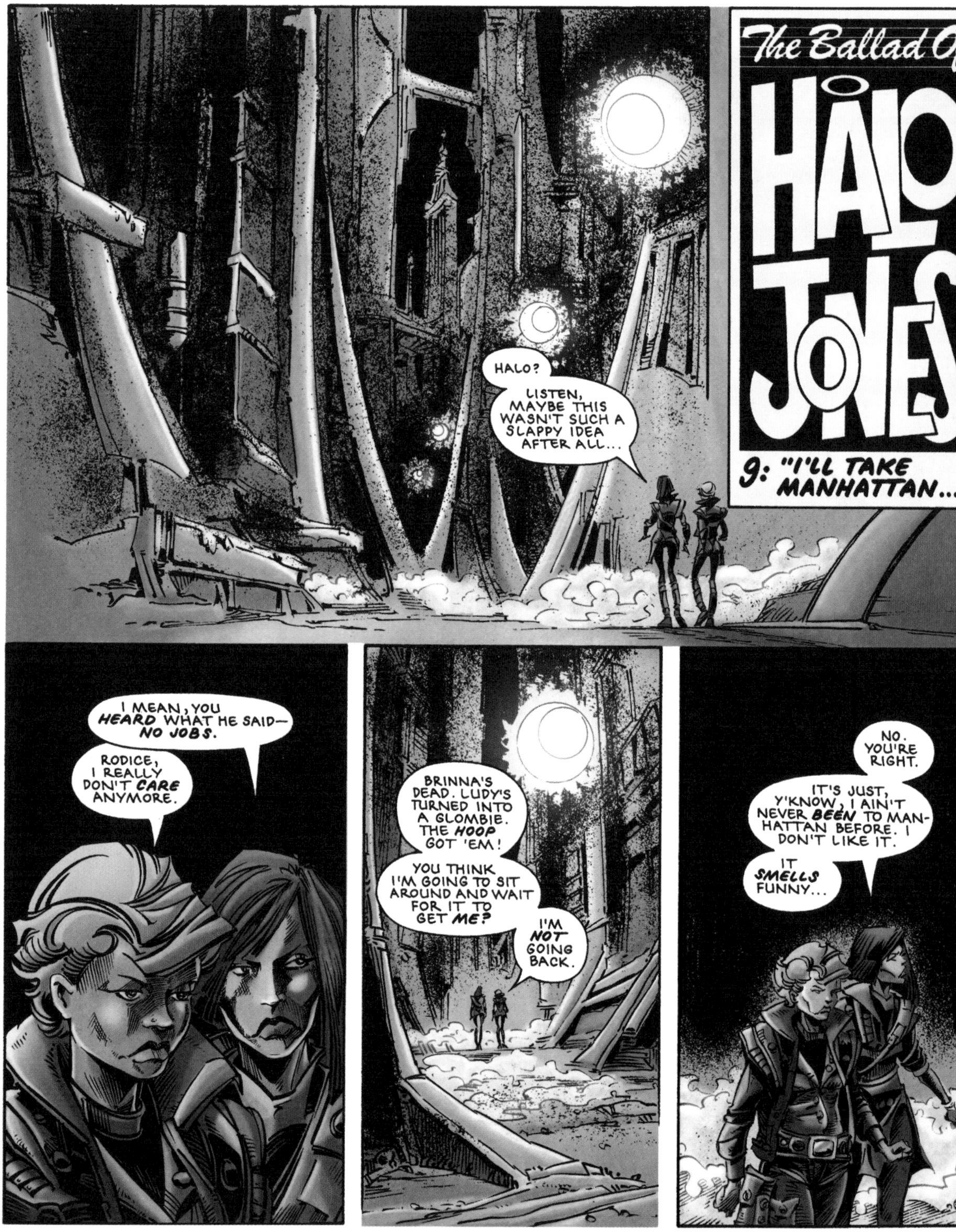
The Ballad Of
HALO JONES
9: "I'LL TAKE MANHATTAN..."
HALO?
LISTEN, MAYBE THIS WASN'T SUCH A SLAPPY IDEA AFTER ALL...
I MEAN, YOU HEARD WHAT HE SAID— NO JOBS.
RODICE, I REALLY DON'T CARE ANYMORE.
BRINNA'S DEAD. LUDY'S TURNED INTO A GLOMBIE. THE HOOP GOT 'EM!
YOU THINK I'M GOING TO SIT AROUND AND WAIT FOR IT TO GET ME?
I'M NOT GOING BACK.
NO. YOU'RE RIGHT.
IT'S JUST, Y'KNOW, I AIN'T NEVER BEEN TO MANHATTAN BEFORE. I DON'T LIKE IT.
IT SMELLS FUNNY...

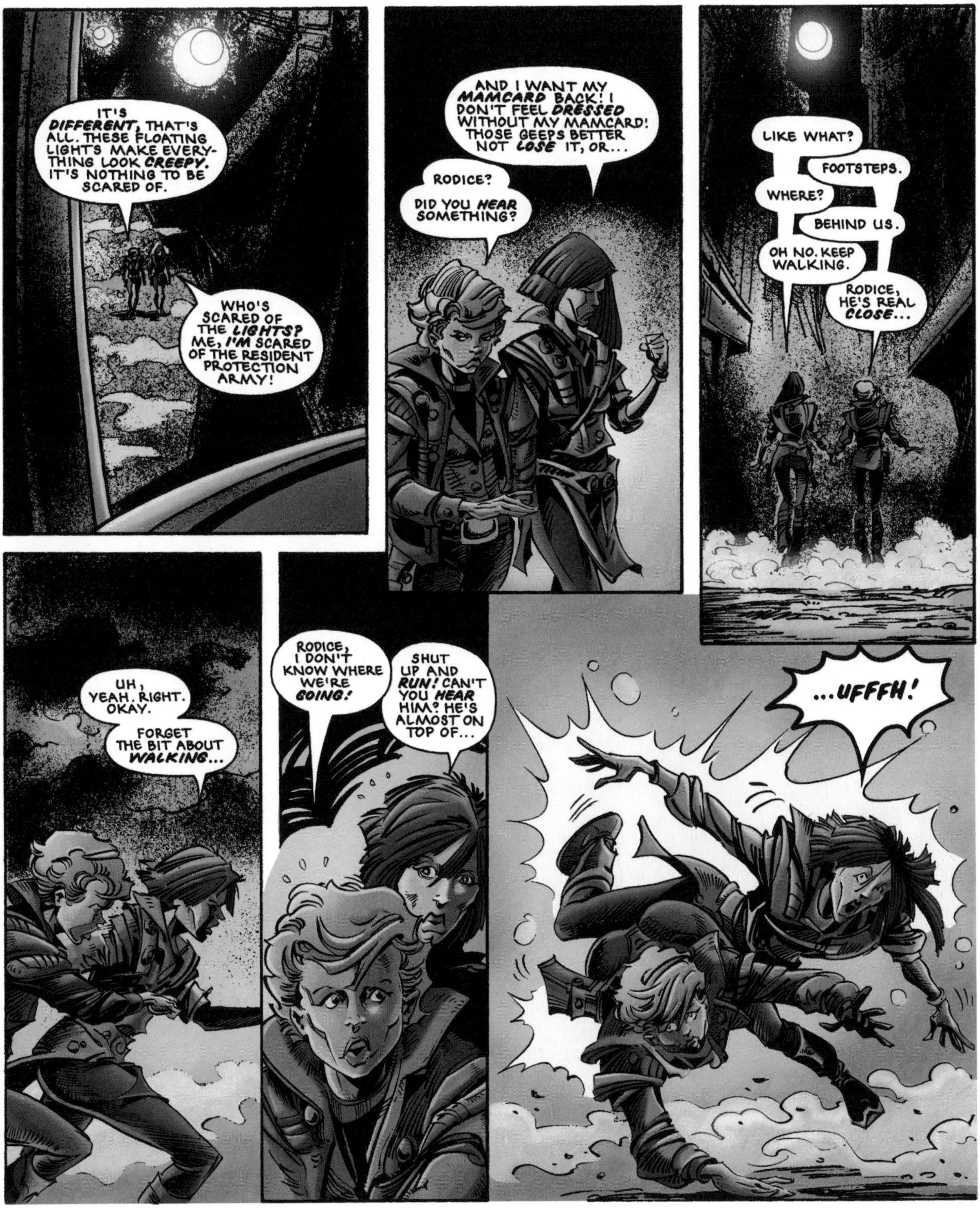

IT'S DIFFERENT, THAT'S ALL. THESE FLOATING LIGHTS MAKE EVERYTHING LOOK CREEPY. IT'S NOTHING TO BE SCARED OF.
WHO'S SCARED OF THE LIGHTS? ME, I'M SCARED OF THE RESIDENT PROTECTION ARMY!
AND I WANT MY MAMCARD BACK! I DON'T FEEL DRESSED WITHOUT MY MAMCARD! THOSE GEEPS BETTER NOT LOSE IT, OR...
RODICE?
DID YOU HEAR SOMETHING?
LIKE WHAT?
FOOTSTEPS.
WHERE?
BEHIND US.
OH NO. KEEP WALKING.
RODICE, HE'S REAL CLOSE...
UH, YEAH. RIGHT. OKAY.
FORGET THE BIT ABOUT WALKING...
RODICE, I DON'T KNOW WHERE WE'RE GOING!
SHUT UP AND RUN! CAN'T YOU HEAR HIM? HE'S ALMOST ON TOP OF...
...UFFFH!

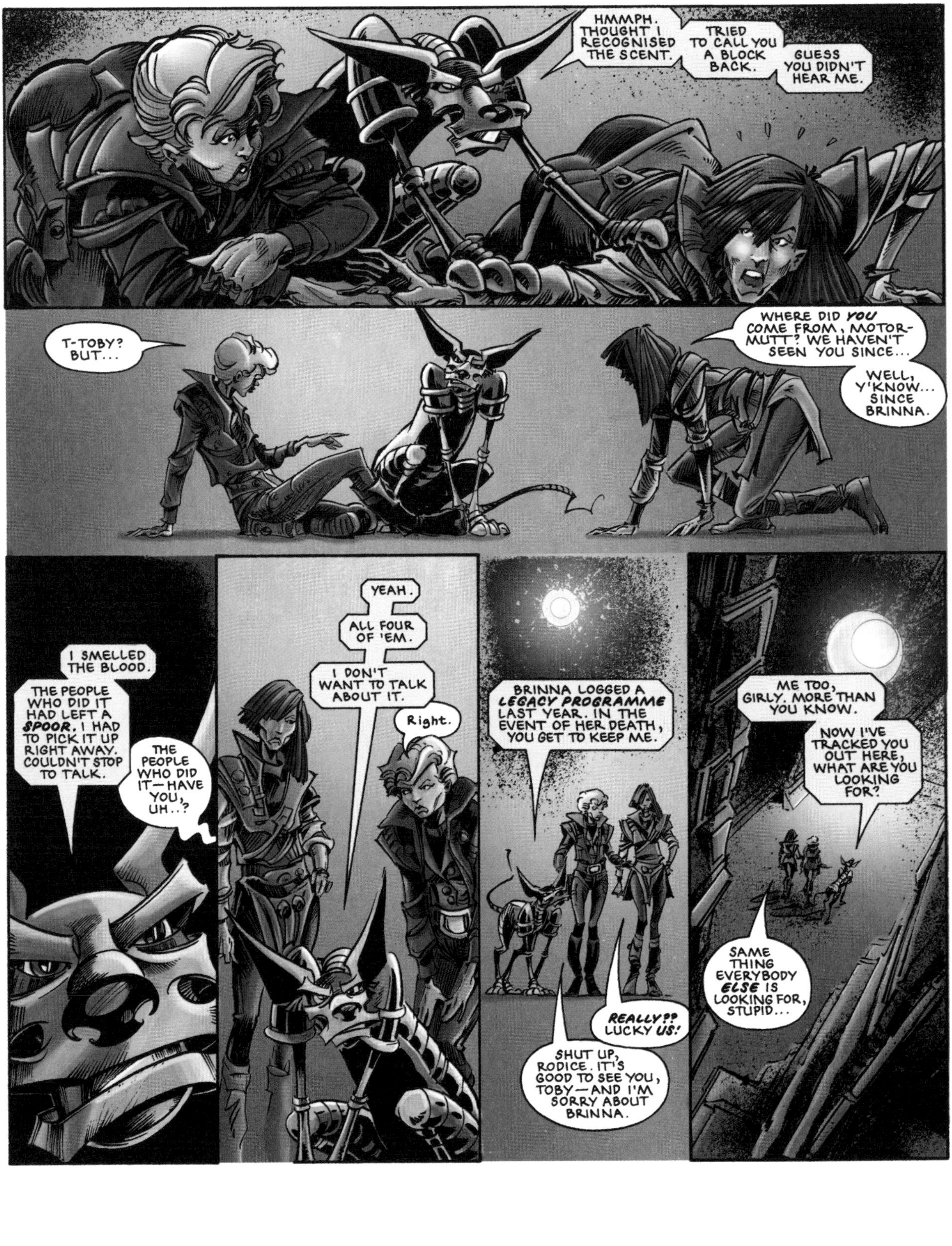
HMMPH. THOUGHT I RECOGNISED THE SCENT.
TRIED TO CALL YOU A BLOCK BACK.
GUESS YOU DIDN'T HEAR ME.
T-TOBY? BUT...
WHERE DID YOU COME FROM, MOTOR-MUTT? WE HAVEN'T SEEN YOU SINCE...
WELL, Y'KNOW... SINCE BRINNA.
I SMELLED THE BLOOD.
THE PEOPLE WHO DID IT HAD LEFT A SPOOR. I HAD TO PICK IT UP RIGHT AWAY. COULDN'T STOP TO TALK.
THE PEOPLE WHO DID IT—HAVE YOU, UH..?
YEAH.
ALL FOUR OF 'EM.
I DON'T WANT TO TALK ABOUT IT.
Right.
BRINNA LOGGED A LEGACY PROGRAMME LAST YEAR. IN THE EVENT OF HER DEATH, YOU GET TO KEEP ME.
REALLY?? LUCKY US!
SHUT UP, RODICE. IT'S GOOD TO SEE YOU, TOBY—AND I'M SORRY ABOUT BRINNA.
ME TOO, GIRLY. MORE THAN YOU KNOW.
NOW I'VE TRACKED YOU OUT HERE, WHAT ARE YOU LOOKING FOR?
SAME THING EVERYBODY ELSE IS LOOKING FOR, STUPID...

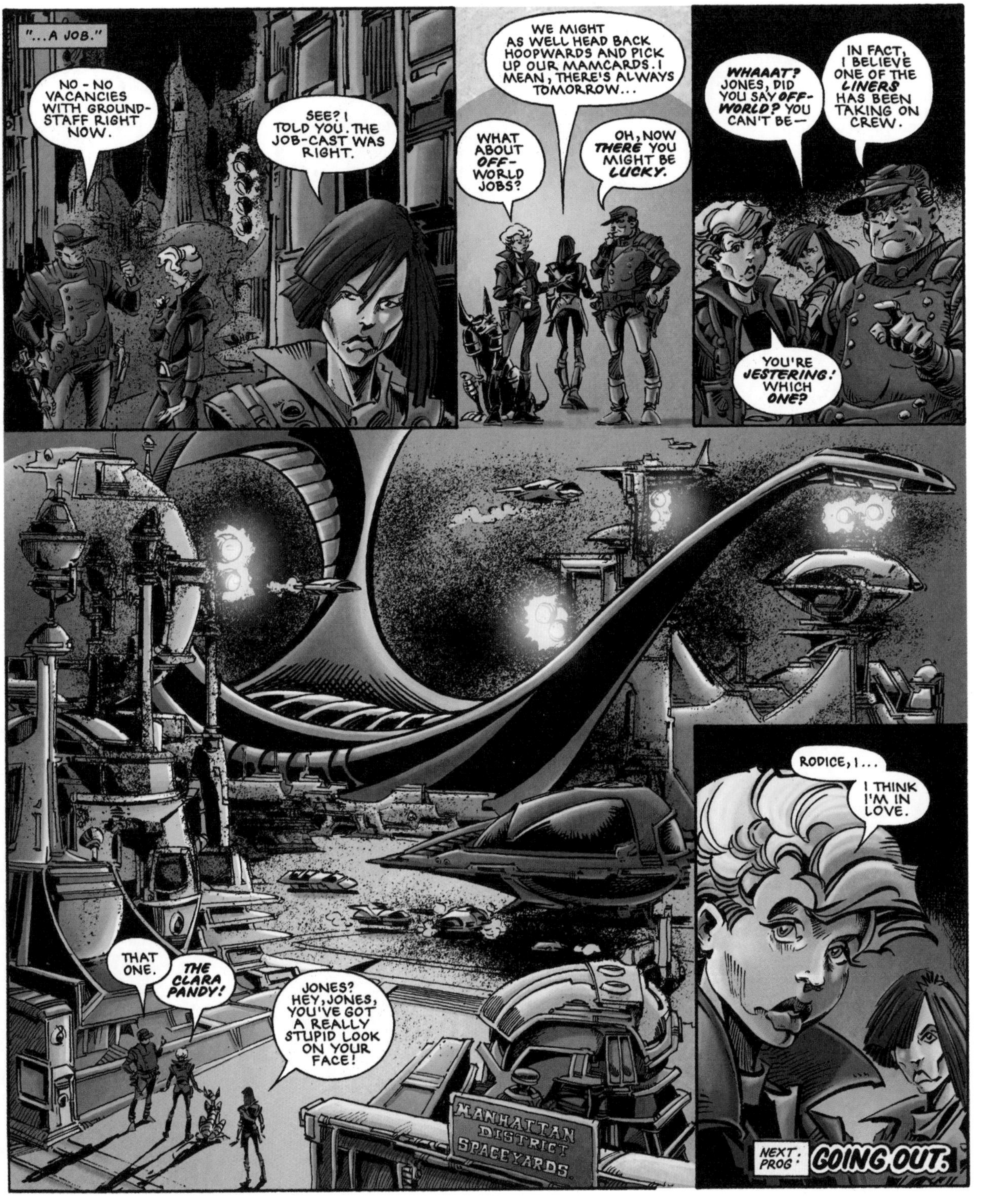

"...A JOB."
NO - NO VACANCIES WITH GROUND-STAFF RIGHT NOW.
SEE? I TOLD YOU. THE JOB-CAST WAS RIGHT.
WE MIGHT AS WELL HEAD BACK HOOPWARDS AND PICK UP OUR MAMCARDS. I MEAN, THERE'S ALWAYS TOMORROW...
WHAT ABOUT OFF-WORLD JOBS?
OH, NOW THERE YOU MIGHT BE LUCKY.
WHAAAT? JONES, DID YOU SAY OFF-WORLD? YOU CAN'T BE—
IN FACT, I BELIEVE ONE OF THE LINERS HAS BEEN TAKING ON CREW.
YOU'RE JESTERING! WHICH ONE?
THAT ONE.
THE CLARA PANDY!
JONES? HEY, JONES, YOU'VE GOT A REALLY STUPID LOOK ON YOUR FACE!
MANHATTAN DISTRICT SPACEYARDS.
RODICE, I...
I THINK I'M IN LOVE.
NEXT PROG: GOING OUT.

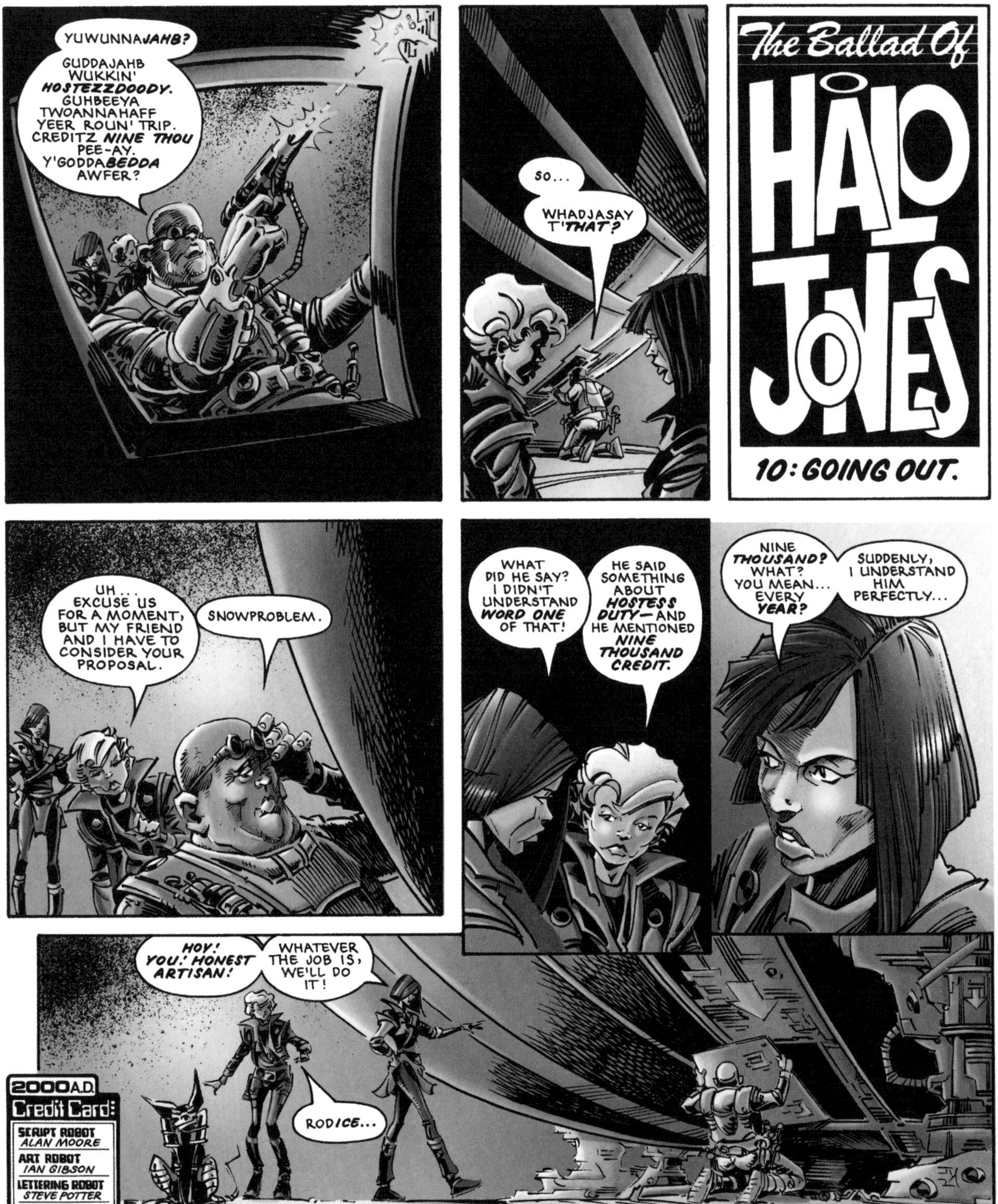
YUWUNNAJAHB?
GUDDAJAHB WUKKIN' HOSTEZZDOODY. GUHBEEYA TWOANNAHAFF YEER ROUN' TRIP. CREDITZ NINE THOU PEE-AY. Y'GODDABEDDA AWFER?
SO...
WHADJASAY T'THAT?
The Ballad Of
HALO JONES
10: GOING OUT.
UH... EXCUSE US FOR A MOMENT, BUT MY FRIEND AND I HAVE TO CONSIDER YOUR PROPOSAL.
SNOWPROBLEM.
WHAT DID HE SAY? I DIDN'T UNDERSTAND WORD ONE OF THAT!
HE SAID SOMETHING ABOUT HOSTESS DUTY— AND HE MENTIONED NINE THOUSAND CREDIT.
NINE THOUSAND? WHAT? YOU MEAN... EVERY YEAR?
SUDDENLY, I UNDERSTAND HIM PERFECTLY...
HOY! YOU! HONEST ARTISAN!
WHATEVER THE JOB IS, WE'LL DO IT!
RODICE...
2000 A.D.
Credit Card:
SCRIPT ROBOT ALAN MOORE
ART ROBOT IAN GIBSON
LETTERING ROBOT STEVE POTTER
COMPU-73E

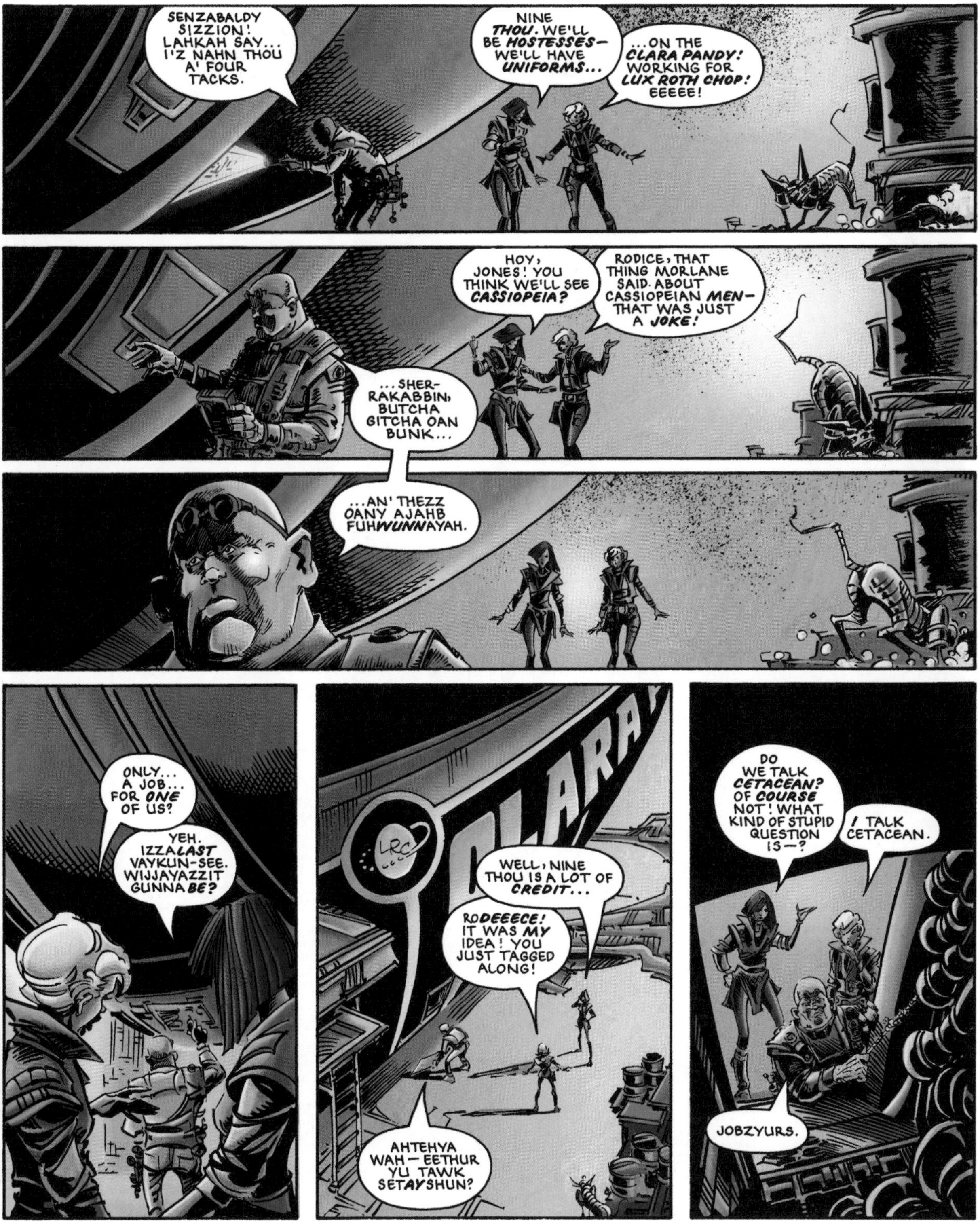

SENZABALDY SIZZION! LAHKAH SAY... I'Z NAHN THOU A' FOUR TACKS.
NINE **THOU**. WE'LL BE **HOSTESSES**— WE'LL HAVE **UNIFORMS**...
...ON THE **CLARA PANDY!** WORKING FOR **LUX ROTH CHOP!** EEEEE!
HOY, JONES! YOU THINK WE'LL SEE **CASSIOPEIA?**
RODICE, THAT THING MORLANE SAID ABOUT CASSIOPEIAN **MEN**— THAT WAS JUST A **JOKE!**
...SHER-RAKABBIN, BUTCHA GITCHA OAN BUNK...
...AN' THEZZ OANY AJAHB FUH**WUNN**AYAH.
ONLY... A JOB... FOR **ONE** OF US?
YEH. IZZA**LAST** VAYKUN-SEE. WIJJAYAZZIT GUNNA **BE?**
CLARA
LRC
WELL, NINE THOU IS A LOT OF **CREDIT...**
RO**DEEECE!** IT WAS **MY** IDEA! YOU JUST TAGGED ALONG!
AHTEHYA WAH— EETHUR YU TAWK SET**AY**SHUN?
DO WE TALK **CETACEAN?** OF **COURSE** NOT! WHAT KIND OF STUPID QUESTION IS—?
I TALK CETACEAN.
JOBZYURS.

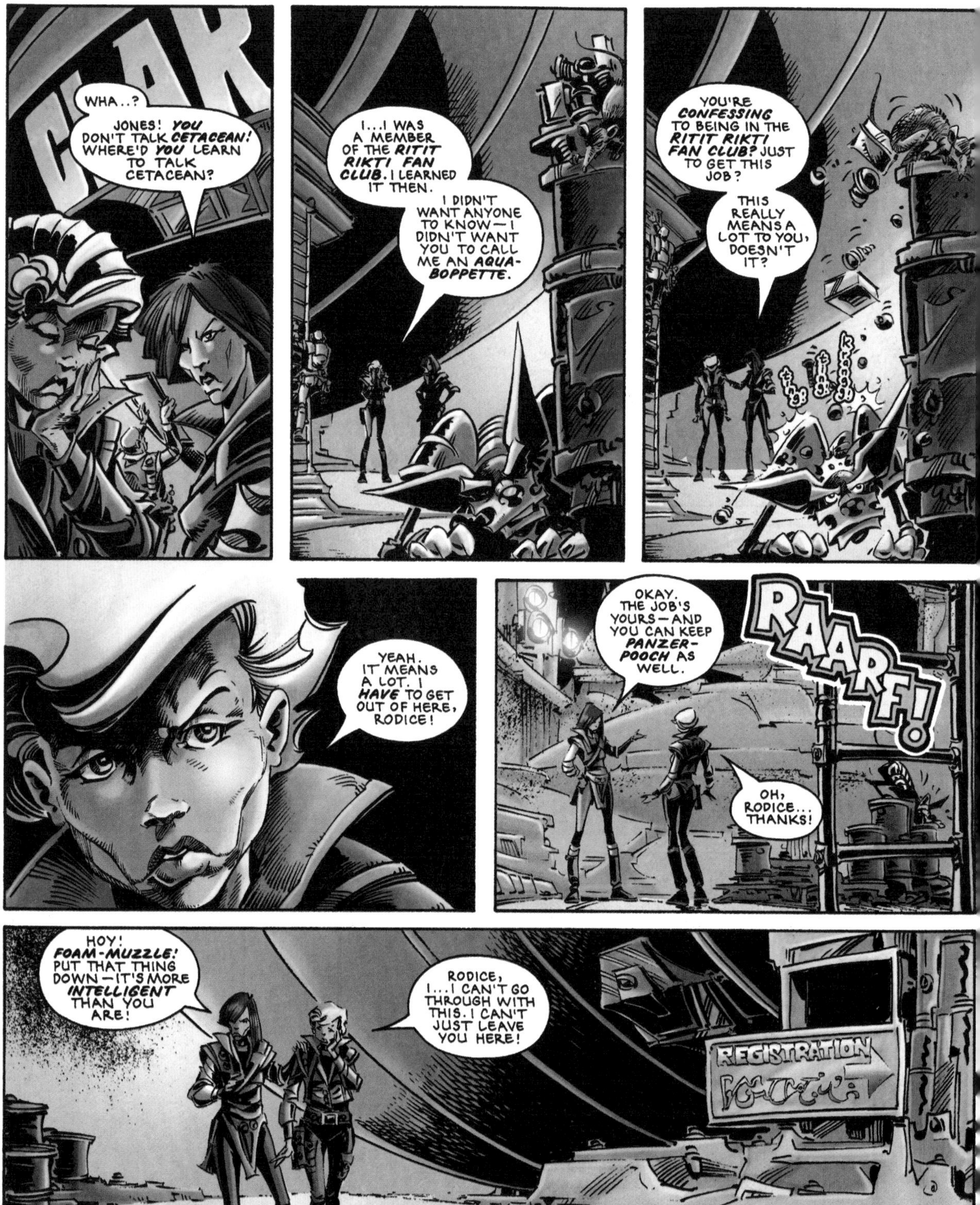

WHA..?
JONES! YOU DON'T TALK CETACEAN! WHERE'D YOU LEARN TO TALK CETACEAN?
I...I WAS A MEMBER OF THE RITIT RIKTI FAN CLUB. I LEARNED IT THEN.
I DIDN'T WANT ANYONE TO KNOW—I DIDN'T WANT YOU TO CALL ME AN AQUA-BOPPETTE.
YOU'RE CONFESSING TO BEING IN THE RITIT RIKTI FAN CLUB? JUST TO GET THIS JOB?
THIS REALLY MEANS A LOT TO YOU, DOESN'T IT?
ting!
ting!
krang!
YEAH. IT MEANS A LOT. I HAVE TO GET OUT OF HERE, RODICE!
OKAY. THE JOB'S YOURS—AND YOU CAN KEEP PANZER-POOCH AS WELL.
RAARF!
OH, RODICE... THANKS!
HOY! FOAM-MUZZLE! PUT THAT THING DOWN—IT'S MORE INTELLIGENT THAN YOU ARE!
RODICE, I...I CAN'T GO THROUGH WITH THIS. I CAN'T JUST LEAVE YOU HERE!
REGISTRATION

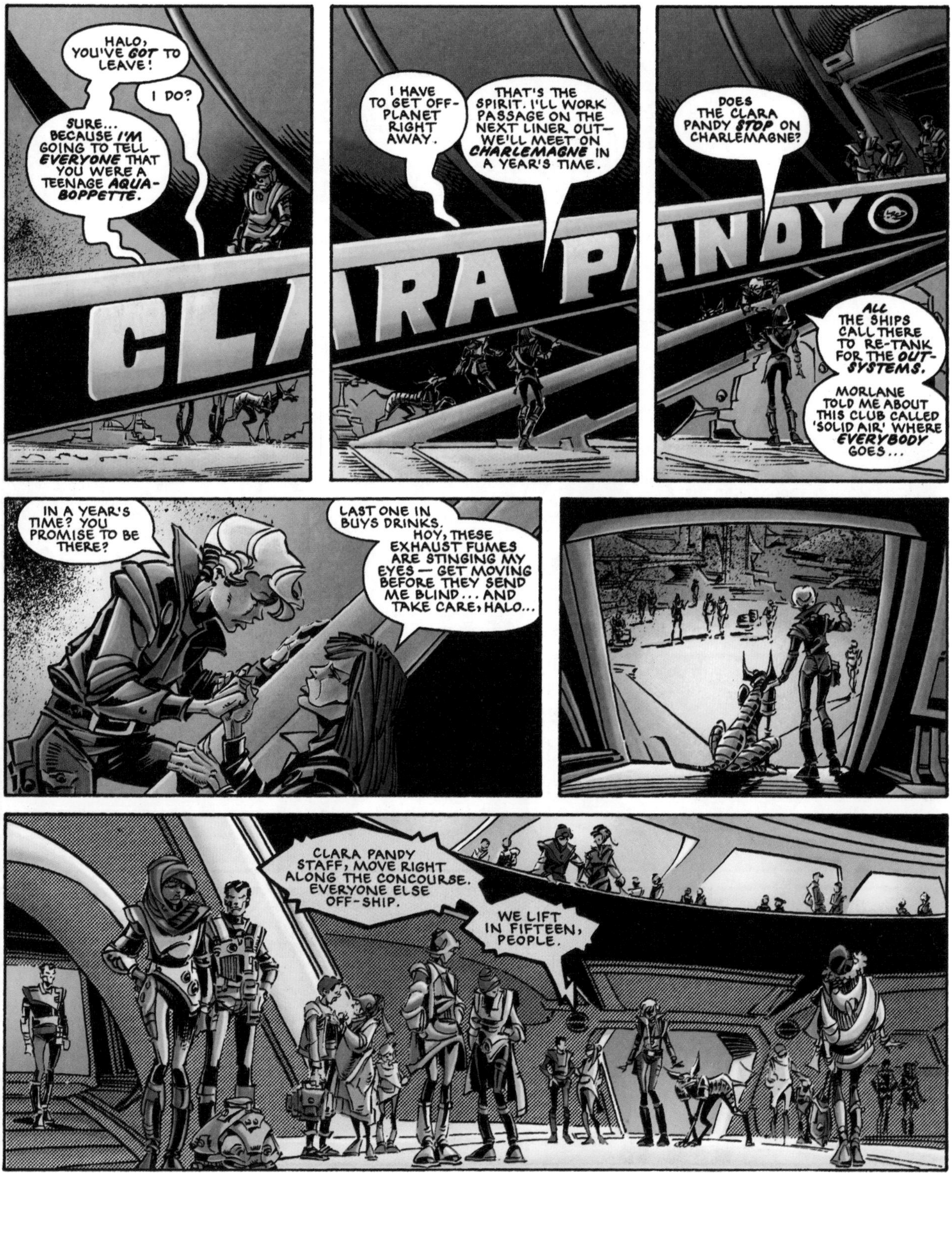
HALO, YOU'VE GOT TO LEAVE!
I DO?
SURE... BECAUSE I'M GOING TO TELL EVERYONE THAT YOU WERE A TEENAGE AQUA-BOPPETTE.
I HAVE TO GET OFF-PLANET RIGHT AWAY.
THAT'S THE SPIRIT. I'LL WORK PASSAGE ON THE NEXT LINER OUT— WE'LL MEET ON CHARLEMAGNE IN A YEAR'S TIME.
CLARA PANDY
DOES THE CLARA PANDY STOP ON CHARLEMAGNE?
ALL THE SHIPS CALL THERE TO RE-TANK FOR THE OUT-SYSTEMS.
MORLANE TOLD ME ABOUT THIS CLUB CALLED 'SOLID AIR' WHERE EVERYBODY GOES...
IN A YEAR'S TIME? YOU PROMISE TO BE THERE?
LAST ONE IN BUYS DRINKS.
HOY, THESE EXHAUST FUMES ARE STINGING MY EYES — GET MOVING BEFORE THEY SEND ME BLIND... AND TAKE CARE, HALO...
CLARA PANDY STAFF, MOVE RIGHT ALONG THE CONCOURSE. EVERYONE ELSE OFF-SHIP.
WE LIFT IN FIFTEEN, PEOPLE.

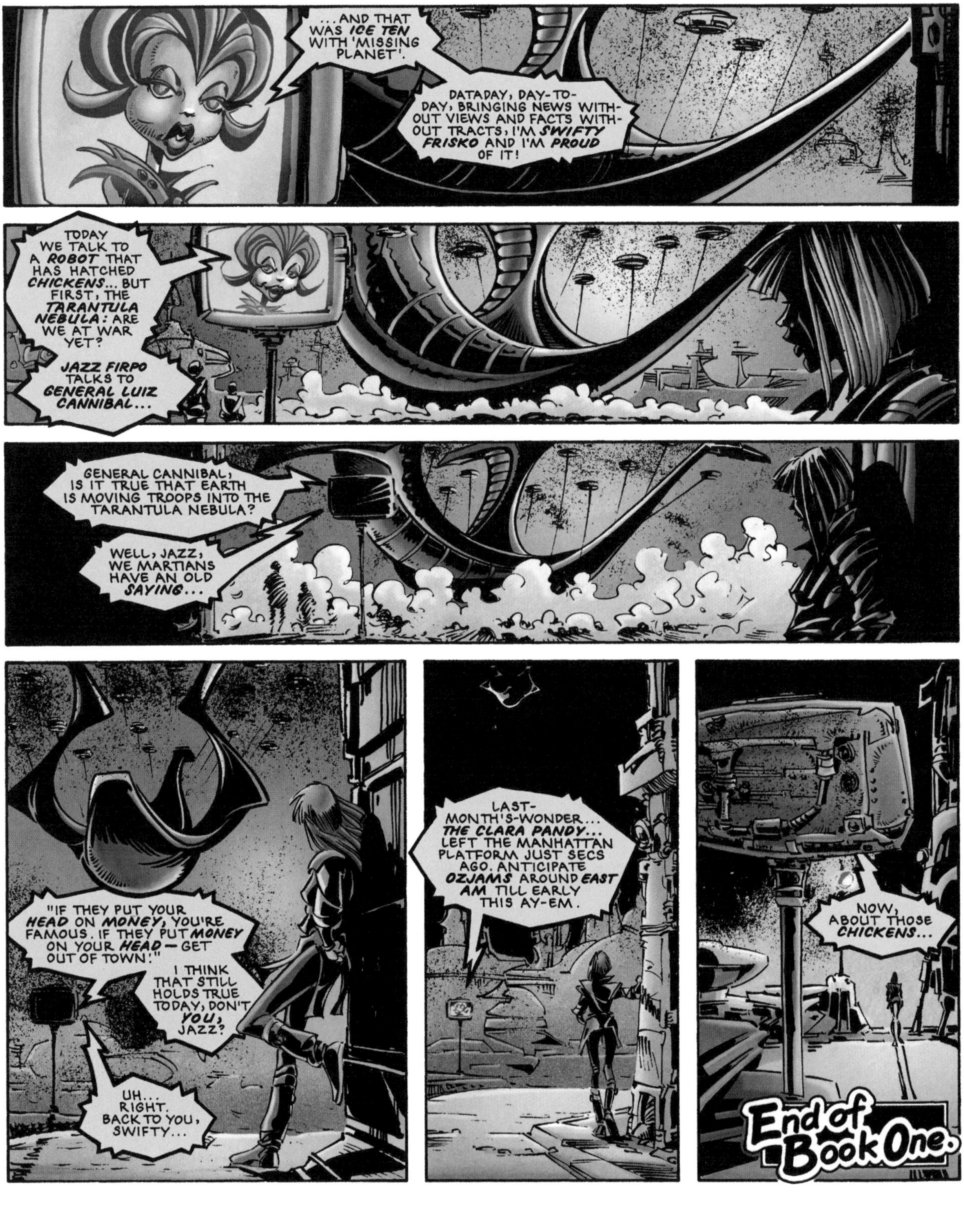
...AND THAT WAS ICE TEN WITH 'MISSING PLANET'.
DATADAY, DAY-TO-DAY, BRINGING NEWS WITHOUT VIEWS AND FACTS WITHOUT TRACTS, I'M SWIFTY FRISKO AND I'M PROUD OF IT!
TODAY WE TALK TO A ROBOT THAT HAS HATCHED CHICKENS... BUT FIRST, THE TARANTULA NEBULA: ARE WE AT WAR YET?
JAZZ FIRPO TALKS TO GENERAL LUIZ CANNIBAL...
GENERAL CANNIBAL, IS IT TRUE THAT EARTH IS MOVING TROOPS INTO THE TARANTULA NEBULA?
WELL, JAZZ, WE MARTIANS HAVE AN OLD SAYING...
"IF THEY PUT YOUR HEAD ON MONEY, YOU'RE FAMOUS. IF THEY PUT MONEY ON YOUR HEAD — GET OUT OF TOWN."
I THINK THAT STILL HOLDS TRUE TODAY, DON'T YOU, JAZZ?
UH... RIGHT. BACK TO YOU, SWIFTY...
LAST-MONTH'S-WONDER... THE CLARA PANDY... LEFT THE MANHATTAN PLATFORM JUST SECS AGO. ANTICIPATE OZJAMS AROUND EAST AM TILL EARLY THIS AY-EM.
NOW, ABOUT THOSE CHICKENS...
End of Book One.

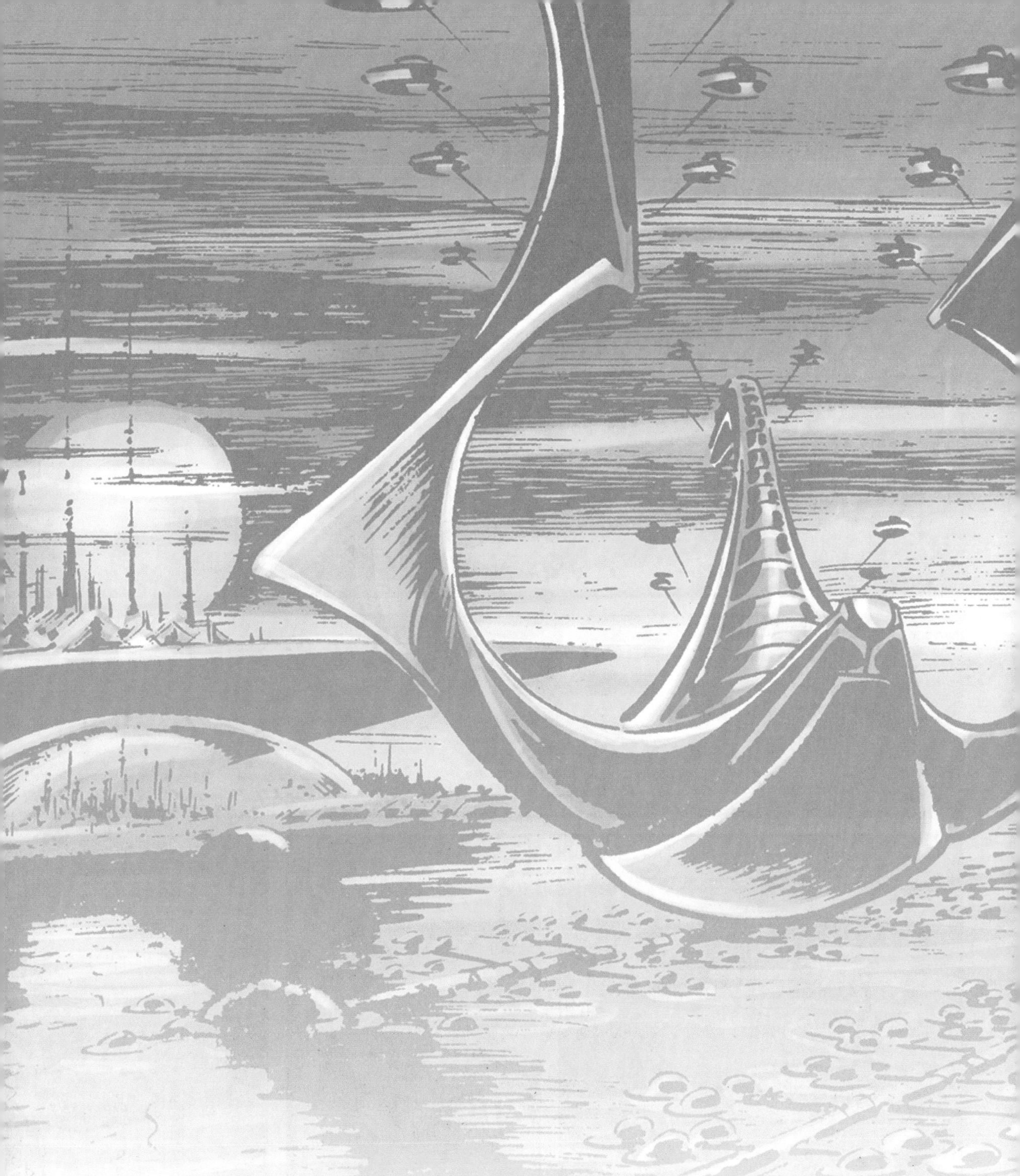

BONUS CONTENT
& COVER GALLERY

GUNS, GUYS AND GORE

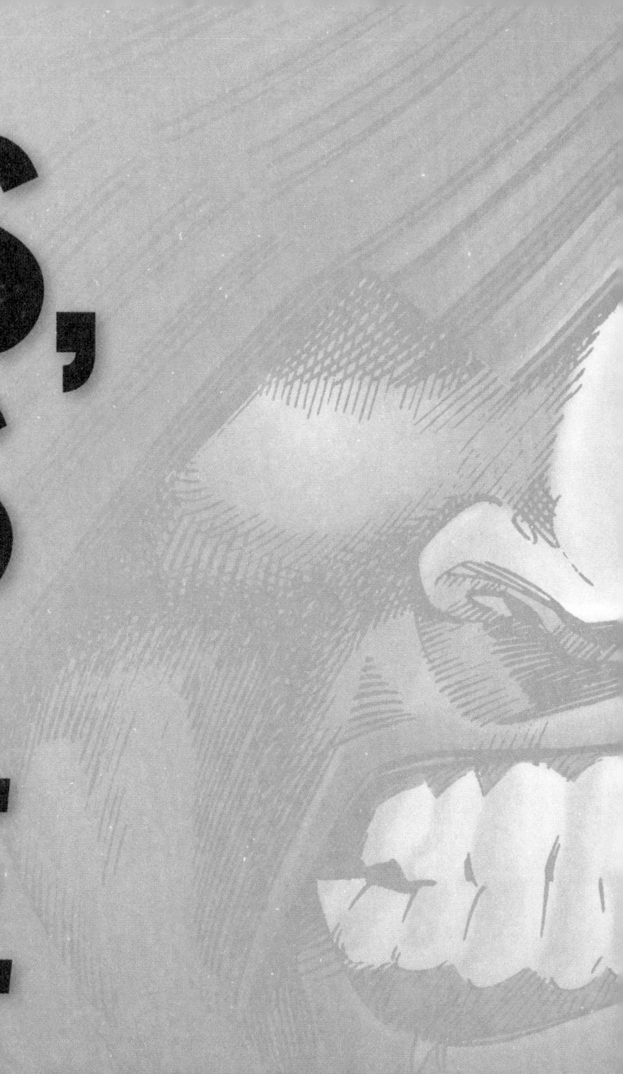

IF I HAD TO SUM UP AS SUCCINCTLY AS POSSIBLE WHAT MAKES A CLASSIC *2000 AD* SERIES, I'D PROBABLY BOIL it down to those three words: Guns, guys and gore (and maybe a few giggles thrown in for good measure). Curious, then, that when asked for the first time to design a series from the ground up for that erstwhile publication I should have opted for ships, squeezes and shopping expeditions. All I can really say in my defence is that it seemed perfectly logical at the time.

I certainly didn't do it out of any inherent dislike for the 'Three G's mentioned above . . . in my admiration for *Judge Dredd, Strontium Dog, Robo Hunter* and all the rest I stand second to no man, feeling that the world in general and *2000 AD* in particular would be a poorer place without them. Rather, I think I was motivated by a desire to fill in some of the holes left between those strips. . . some thing that would complement the pervasive flavour of cordite and carnage and which would give the reader something to clean his or her palate with in between the meat courses.

Written at a time when most of the IPC girls comics line seemed to be heading for that last great midnight feast in the dorm and given that *2000 AD* has a larger female readership than any British boy's comic has a right to expect, it seemed appropriate that the strip should be about women. I didn't want to write about a pretty scatterbrain who fainted a lot and had trouble keeping her clothes on. I similarily had no inclination to unleash yet another Tough Bitch With A Disintegrator And An Extra 'Y'Chromosome upon the world. What I wanted was simply an ordinary woman such as you might find standing in front of you while queuing for the check-out at Tesco's, but transposed to the sort of future environment that seemed a pre-requisite of what was, after all, a boy's science fiction comic. Hence, *The Ballad of Halo Jones*.

Having decided upon the broad list of ingredients outlined above, choosing an artist for the strip was sublimely easy: It had to be Ian Gibson. There were six reasons for this. Firstly, he was available. Secondly, he draws incredibly good women. Thirdly, I'd been dying

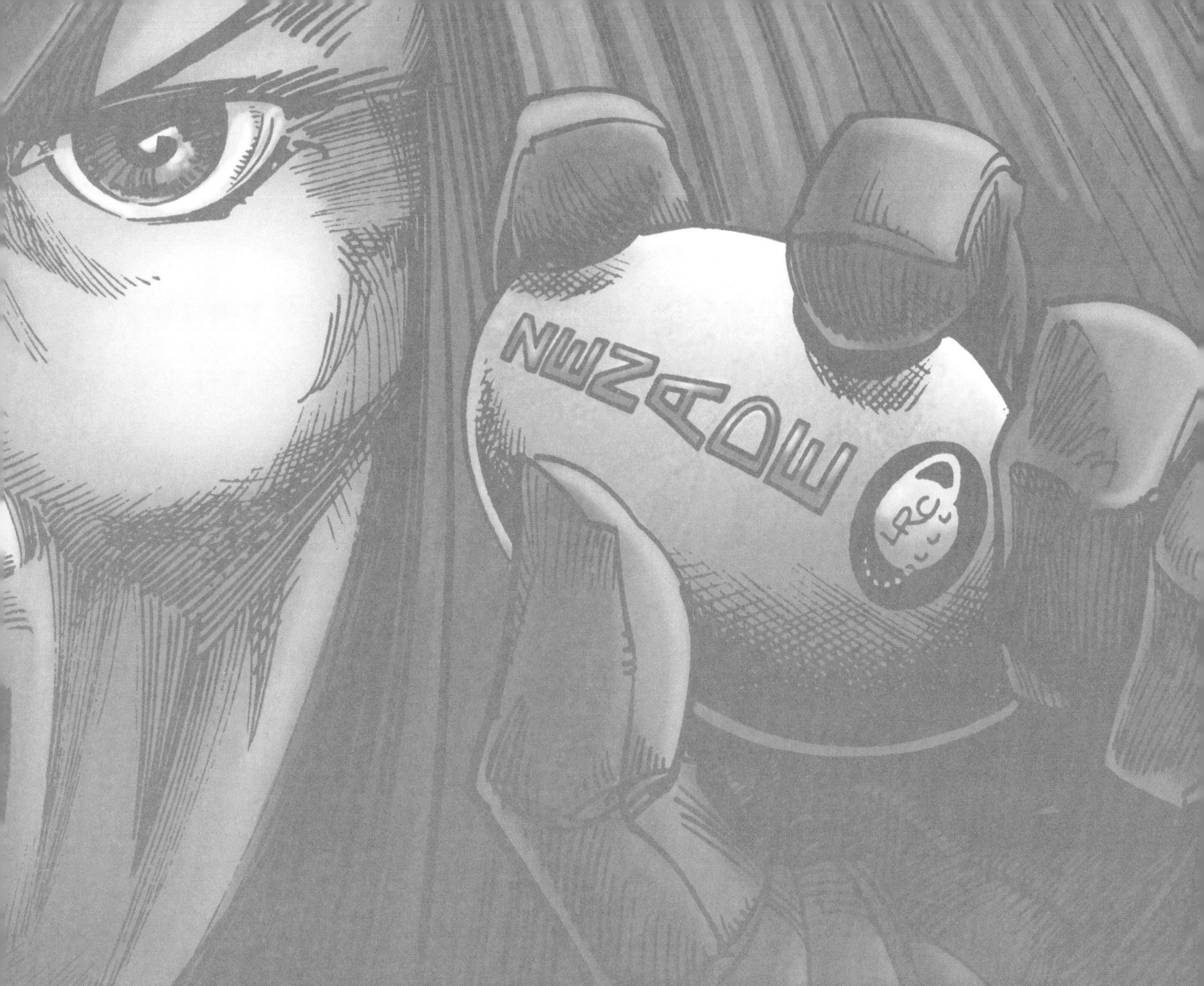

to work with Ian again ever since our one and only collaborative Future Shock (*Grawks Bearing Gifts*). Fourthly, he's very accomplished when it comes to drawing women. Fifthly, he has the sort of fertile, brimming imagination that would prove invaluable on a strip with as much intricate social detail as Halo Jones. Sixthly, his women are something else.

Once Ian was safely on board, the two of us proceeded to work out the fine details of our central character and her environment. We designed the world, its political make up, its principal diet, its language and its dress standards, with Ian providing as many of the main concepts and the small touches as I myself. Did you know, for example, that the strange Esperanto-like language in which many of the Hoop's street signs are lettered as an alternative to English is actually a real, workable alternate language that Ian had designed for fun some years earlier? Or that it was Ian who solved the problem of coming up with a sensible and practical form of dress for the strip's main alien race, the armless Proximen?

Naturally, given its nature, the strip wasn't really for everyone. Some found our decision to dump the reader straight in at the deep end with a totally alien society and let them figure things out for themselves to be merely confusing and irritating. Then, of course, there were those readers who complained that very little happened in the strip. Personally, I think what they actually meant was that very little violence happened in the strip, but then it was their twenty four pee a week, and they have every right to be bored if they damn well want to be. In short, for numerous reasons, not every body liked Halo Jones Book One.

But we did. And the people at *2000 AD* did. And if you've paid out good money for the volume you hold in your hands, then the chances are that you did too. As for everyone else, I really only have one question:

What's the matter? Don't you like girls?

Alan Moore
July 1986

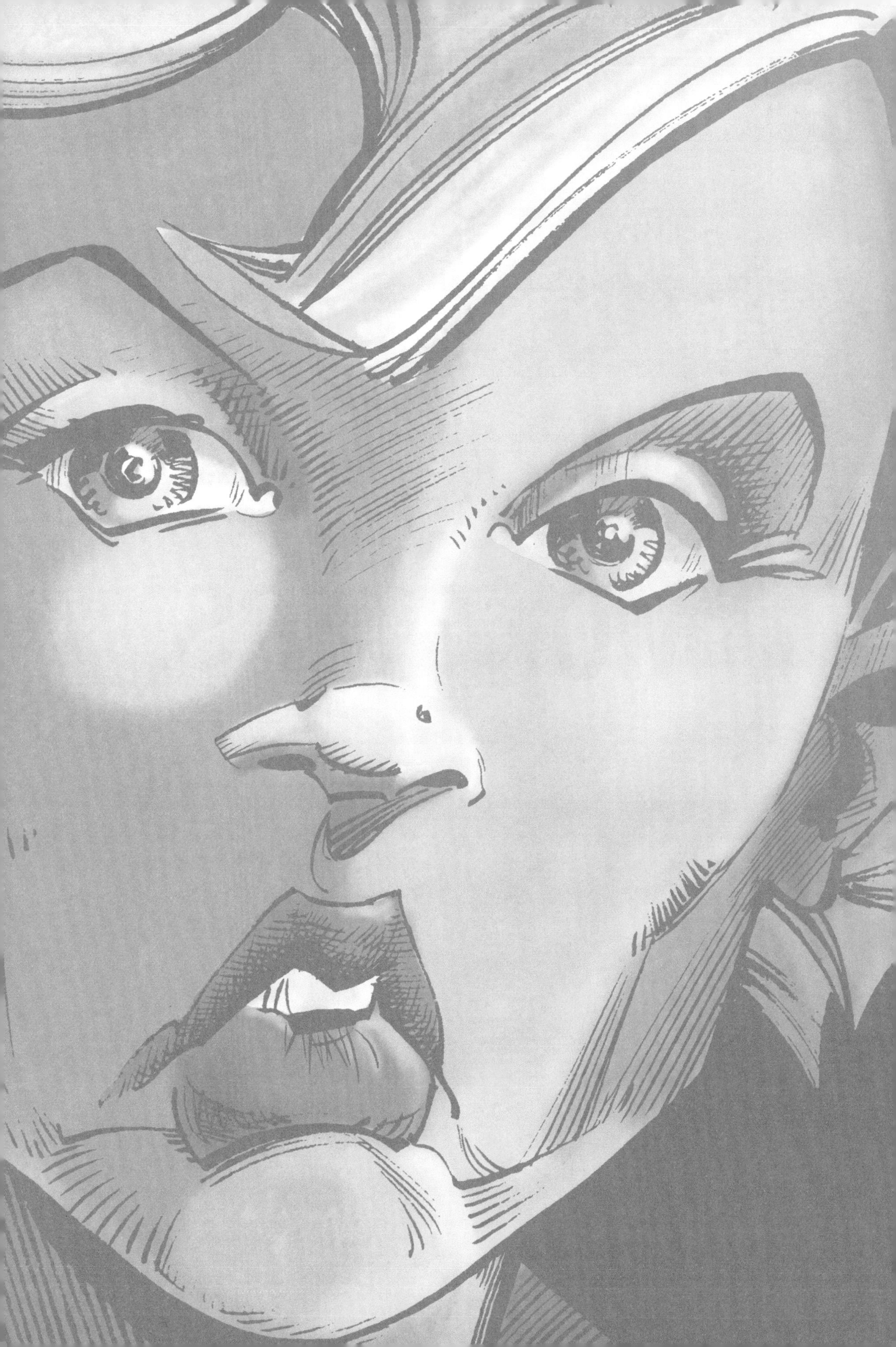

GIRLS, ROCKETS
AND MONSTERS...

IT WAS AT A TITAN 'POST-SIGNING' PARTY THAT THE IDEA FOR THE STORY ACTUALLY STARTED. I'D WANTED to work with Alan for some time, ever since reading his excellent Skizz story in 2000 AD, complemented by Jim Baikie's wonderful illustrations. So when the chance arose, I was quick to pounce on it. I started off by asking Steve MacManus, the then editor of *2000 AD*, if he'd be happy for Alan and I to work together on a new story. Steve said he was. Even back then, I remember I specified a 'girl's story', and one that actually showed some respect for women for a change. I next talked to Alan, who was similarly happy with the idea. He mulled it over for a while and came back full of enthusiasm, telling Steve that he had all the important ingredients... "Girls, rockets and monsters!" Everyone liked the recipe at once, and so Halo was born.

Alan and I had many long discussions about the whole story concept, the characterisations, and where we were taking Halo over the projected nine (!) books of the series. A lot of the internal workings of Halo's world I remember that Alan had left mostly to me. At length, I explained to Alan the structure of the Hoop, so that he could incorporate it into his scripts. As ever, he did so with consummate skill. There are certainly plenty of stories for another time, perhaps even for an introduction to book four?

In the meantime, I'd just like to say thanks to Alan for the incredible scripts, thank Steve for taking a chance in the first place and thank Titan for providing the synchronistic link.

Ian Gibson,
Brighton, April 2001

HOOPLIFE

Dataday, day-to-day, I'm *Swifty Frisko*, love me or leave me! If you're one of the jobless of New York State Municipality, then ***the Hoop*** is for ***you***! Tethered conveniently just off the Manhattan Peninsula, it provides a floating haven for its many residents — ***Increased Leisure Citizens*** who dwell in the picturesque Blister-Homes blossoming from the numerous Lilo-Pads adjoining the Hoop.

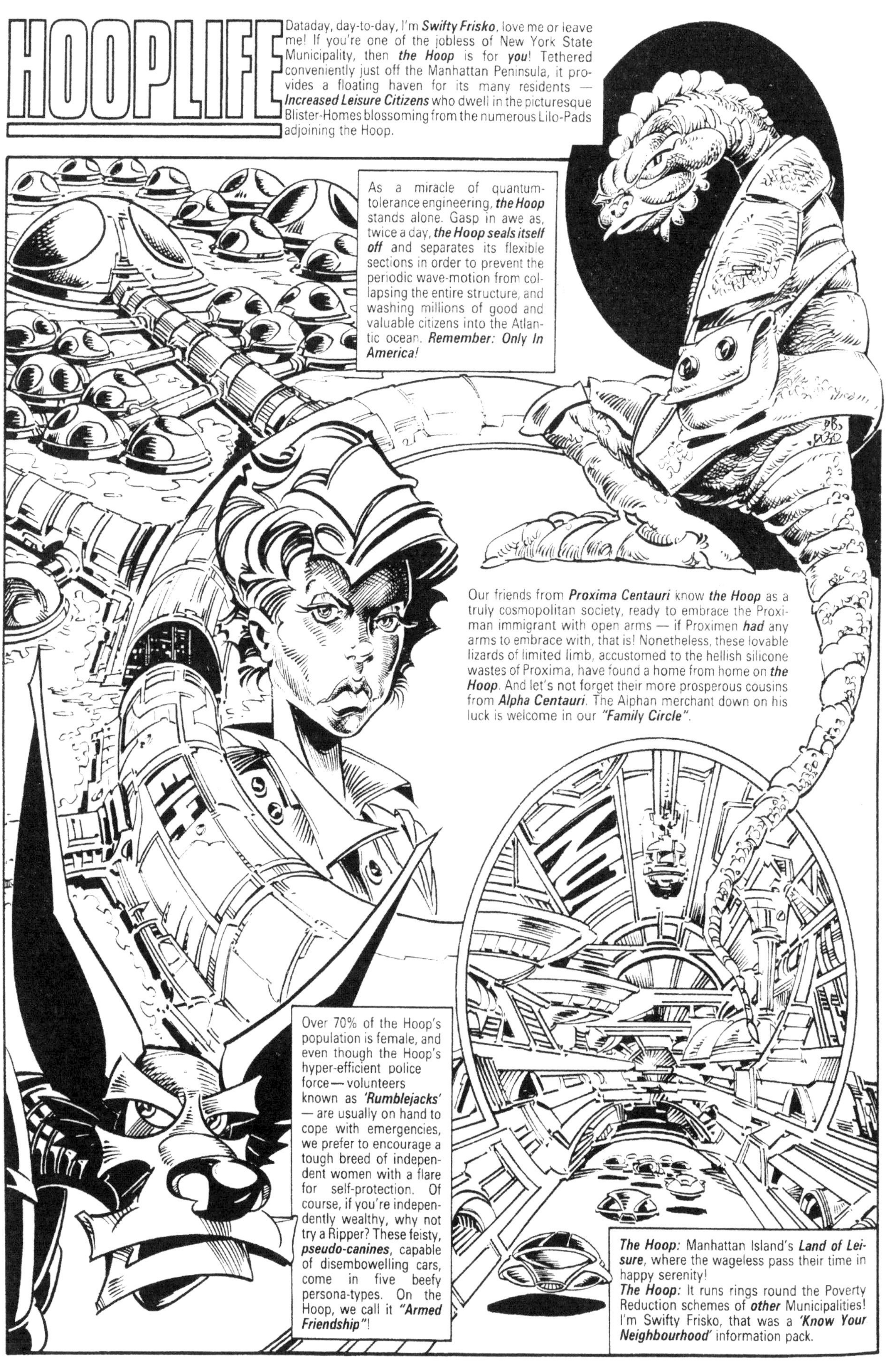

As a miracle of quantum-tolerance engineering, ***the Hoop*** stands alone. Gasp in awe as, twice a day, ***the Hoop seals itself off*** and separates its flexible sections in order to prevent the periodic wave-motion from collapsing the entire structure, and washing millions of good and valuable citizens into the Atlantic ocean. ***Remember: Only In America!***
Our friends from ***Proxima Centauri*** know ***the Hoop*** as a truly cosmopolitan society, ready to embrace the Proximan immigrant with open arms — if Proximen ***had*** any arms to embrace with, that is! Nonetheless, these lovable lizards of limited limb, accustomed to the hellish silicone wastes of Proxima, have found a home from home on ***the Hoop***. And let's not forget their more prosperous cousins from ***Alpha Centauri***. The Alphan merchant down on his luck is welcome in our ***"Family Circle"***.
Over 70% of the Hoop's population is female, and even though the Hoop's hyper-efficient police force — volunteers known as ***'Rumblejacks'*** — are usually on hand to cope with emergencies, we prefer to encourage a tough breed of independent women with a flare for self-protection. Of course, if you're independently wealthy, why not try a Ripper? These feisty, ***pseudo-canines***, capable of disembowelling cars, come in five beefy persona-types. On the Hoop, we call it ***"Armed Friendship"***!
The Hoop: Manhattan Island's ***Land of Leisure***, where the wageless pass their time in happy serenity!
The Hoop: It runs rings round the Poverty Reduction schemes of ***other*** Municipalities!
I'm Swifty Frisko, that was a ***'Know Your Neighbourhood'*** information pack.

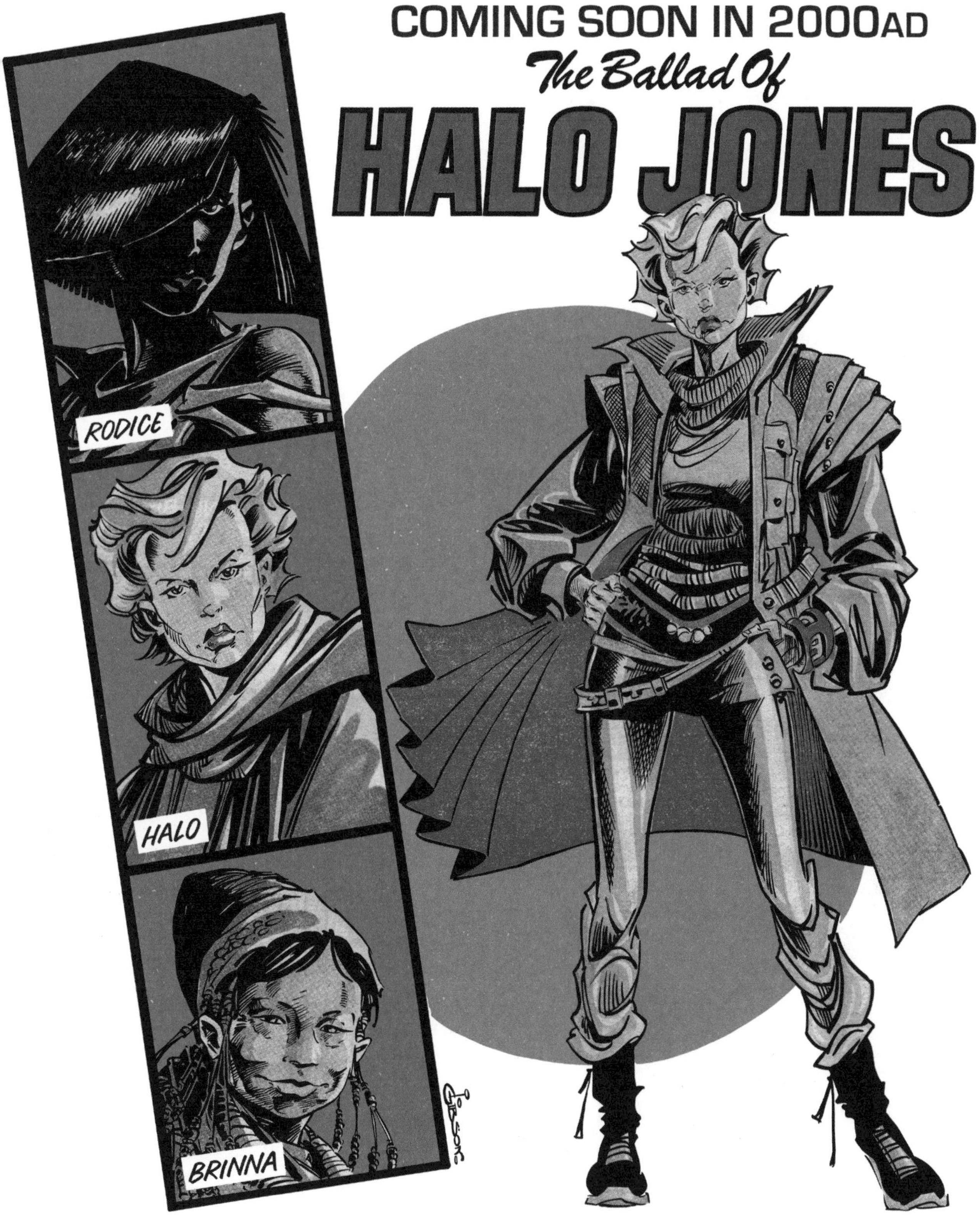
COMING SOON IN 2000AD
The Ballad Of
HALO JONES
RODICE
HALO
BRINNA
GIBSON

Pin-up by **Ian Gibson**

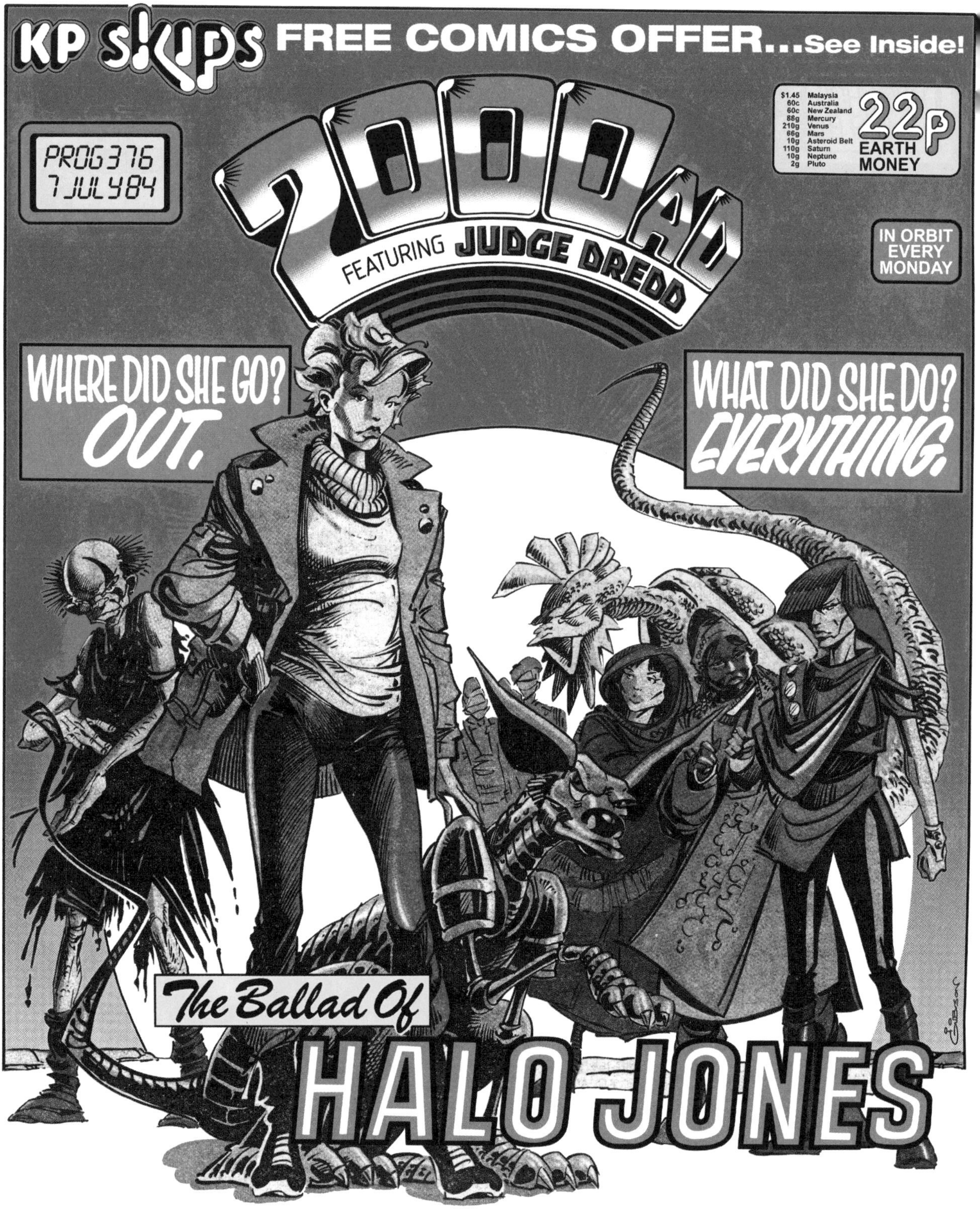
KP SKIPS FREE COMICS OFFER...See Inside!
PROG 376
7 JULY 84
$1.45 Malaysia
60c Australia
60c New Zealand
88g Mercury
210g Venus
66g Mars
10g Asteroid Belt
110g Saturn
10g Neptune
2g Pluto
22p
EARTH MONEY
2000 AD
FEATURING JUDGE DREDD
IN ORBIT EVERY MONDAY
WHERE DID SHE GO? OUT.
WHAT DID SHE DO? EVERYTHING.
The Ballad Of
HALO JONES
GIBSON

2000 AD Prog 376: Cover by **Ian Gibson**

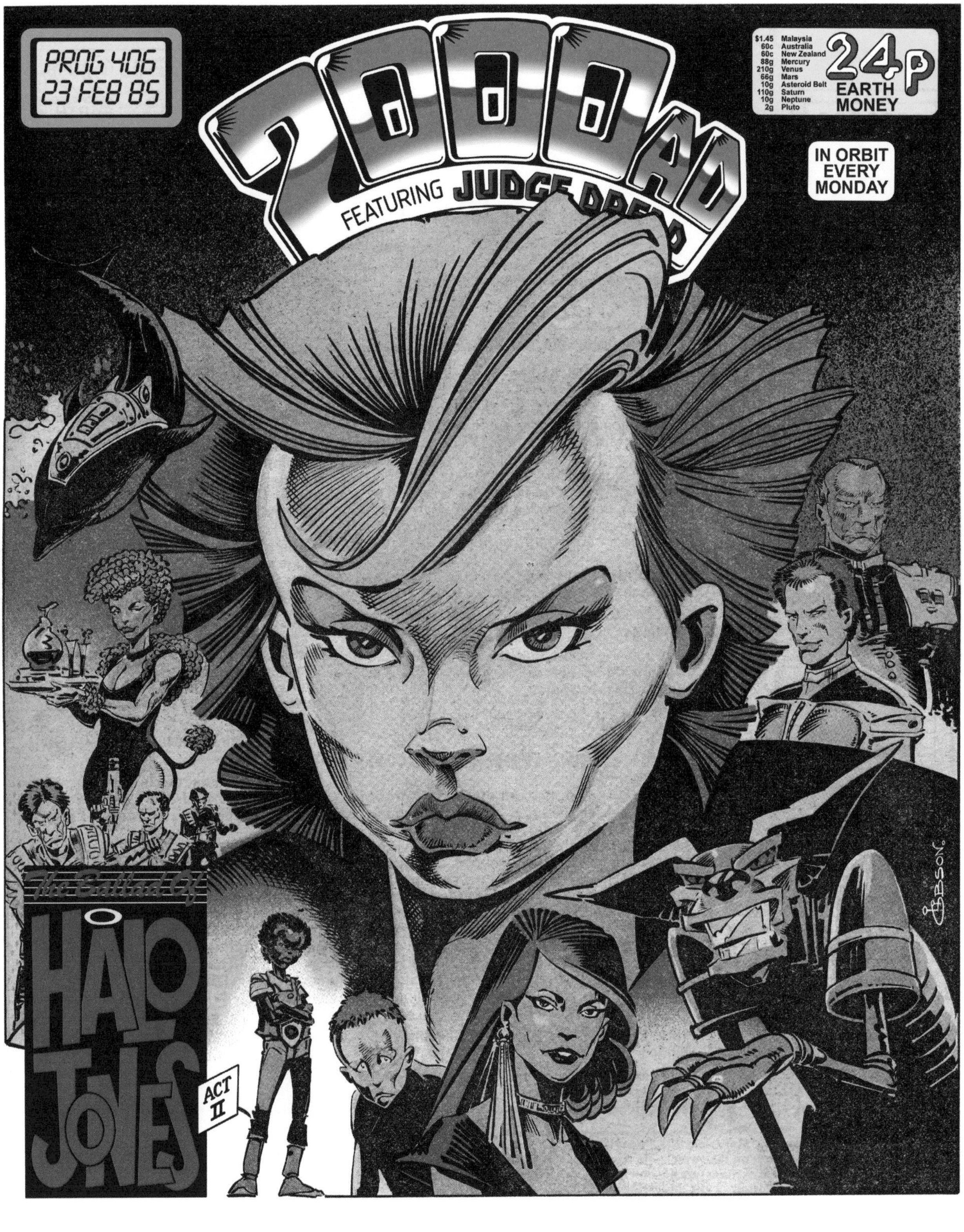
PROG 406
23 FEB 85
2000 AD
FEATURING JUDGE DREDD
$1.45 Malaysia
60c Australia
60c New Zealand
88g Mercury
210g Venus
66g Mars
10g Asteroid Belt
110g Saturn
10g Neptune
2g Pluto
24p
EARTH MONEY
IN ORBIT EVERY MONDAY
The Ballad of
HALO JONES
ACT II
GIBSON

2000 AD Prog 406: Cover by **Ian Gibson**

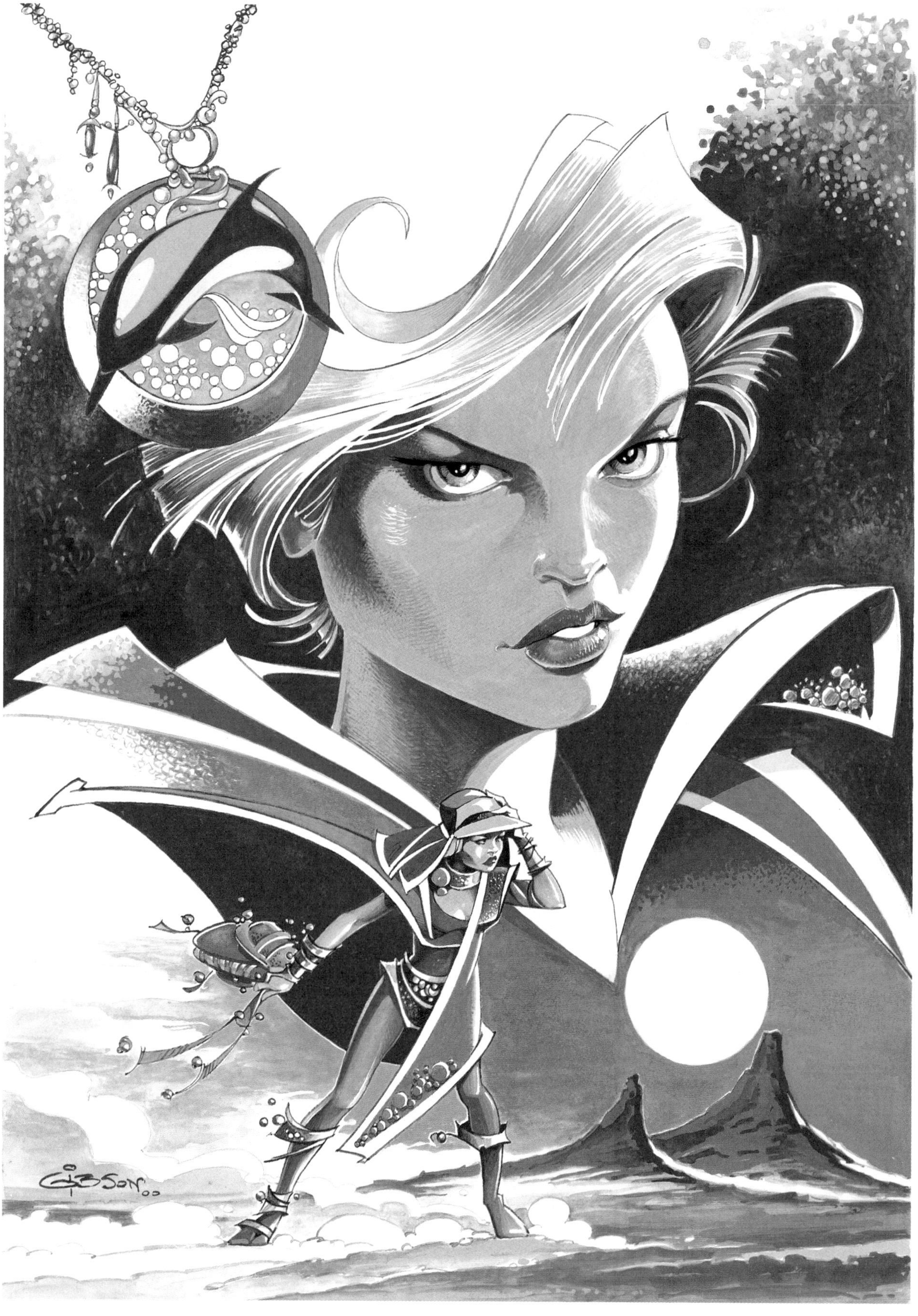
GIBSON

Cover by **Ian Gibson**

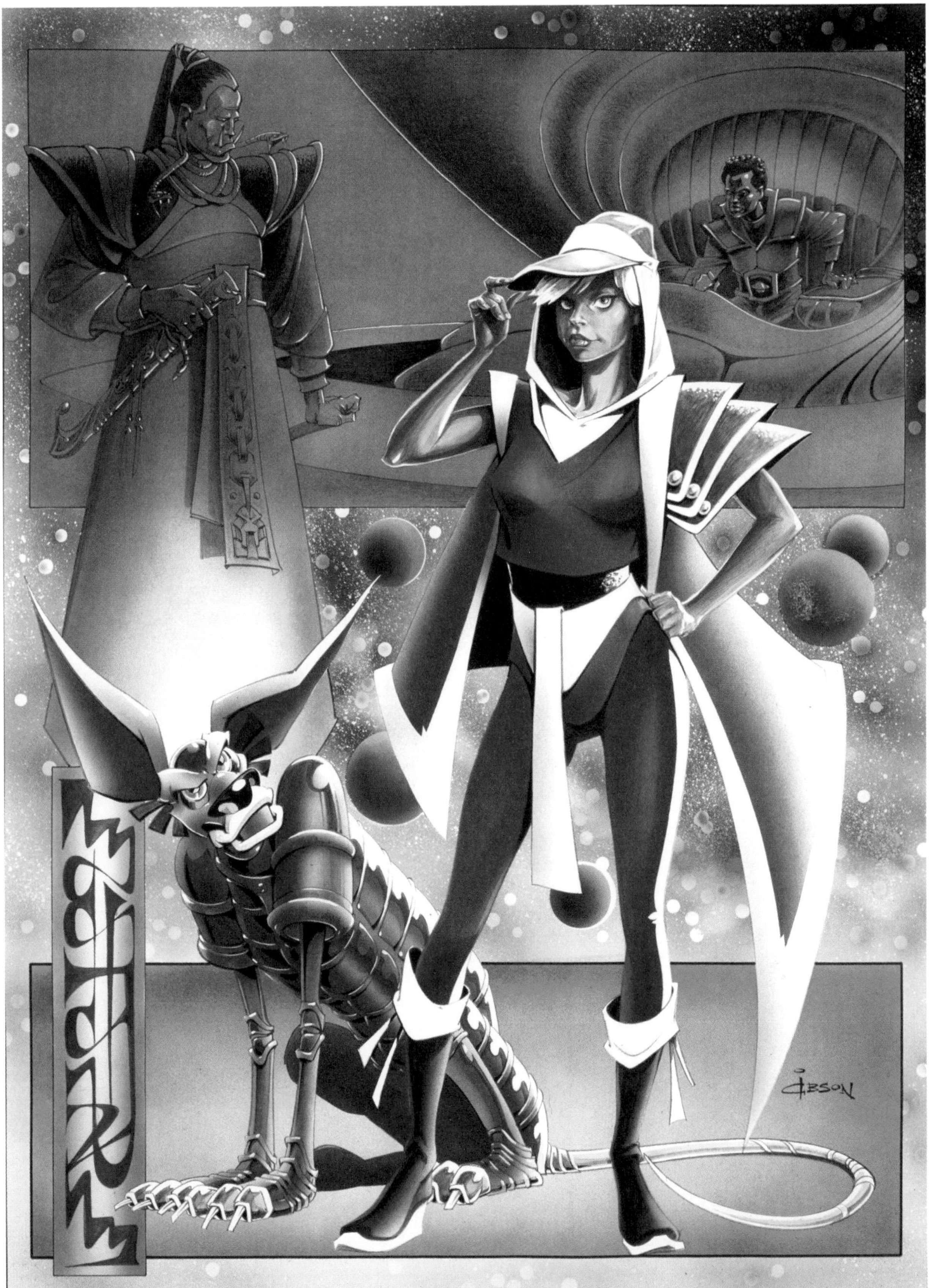
GIBSON

Cover by **Ian Gibson**

ALAN MOORE

One of the most respected and well-known comic writers of the past few decades, Alan Moore created some of *2000 AD's* most popular series, including *Abelard Snazz*, *The Ballad of Halo Jones*, *D.R. & Quinch* and *Skizz*. He has also worked on several other strips for *2000 AD*, most notably *Tharg's Futureshocks*.

Outside of the Galaxy's Greatest Comic, Moore is best known for his work on *Watchmen*, which redefined the superhero genre in 1986, but this is simply touching the surface of a career which has included *Batman*, *Captain Britain*, *From Hell*, *Glory*, *Green Lantern Corps*, *Lost Girls*, *Miracleman*, *A Small Killing*, *Swamp Thing*, *Superman*, *V For Vendetta*, *Promethea* and *The League of Extraordinary Gentlemen*.

More recently his latest novel, *Jerusalem*, was published to critical acclaim.

IAN GIBSON

One of *2000 AD's* best-loved and most honoured artists, Ian Gibson is responsible for the co-creation of *The Ballad of Halo Jones* (with Alan Moore), and created *Bella Bagley*, an unfortunate character in *Judge Dredd's* world who fell head-over-heels in love with 'Old Stoney Face' himself! His work outside the Galaxy's Greatest Comic includes *Chronicles of Genghis Grimtoad*, *Star Wars: Boba Fett*, *X-Men Unlimited*, plus the designs for the TV series *Reboot*.